Theatrical
CHICAGO

RADIO'S 'KENTUCKY MOUNTAIN BOY' BRADLEY KINCAID

by Loyal Jones

Music Transcribed by
John M. Forbes

Introduction by
Archie Green

Appalachian Center/
Berea College

Library of Congress Catalog Card Number 80-26235
ISBN 0-935680-03-9

LIBRARY OF CONGRESS CATALOGING IN PUBLICATION DATA
Jones, Loyal, 1928–
Radio's "Kentucky mountain boy" Bradley Kincaid.
"A selection of Bradley Kincaid's songs": p. 82
Bibliography: p. 186
Discography: p. 171
1. Kincaid, Bradley. 2. Singers–Kentucky–Biography. 3. Folk-songs, American–Kentucky. 4. Ballads, American–Kentucky. I. Title.
ML420.K468J6 784.5'2'00924 [B] 80-26235

Cover and title page designed by Jonathan Greene

For Bradley and his fans,
who know the good songs

CONTENTS

PREFACE

As a farmboy in the North Carolina mountains, I first heard Bradley Kincaid sing from the Grand Ole Opry over our old battery-powered Silvertone. I would often stay up past my bedtime to hear Bradley sing such songs as "Barbara Allen," "The Fatal Rose of Red," "Fair Ellen," and "Froggie Went a-Courtin'." Many years later when I was responsible for programs at conferences of the Council of the Southern Mountains, I rediscovered Bradley in Springfield, Ohio, and invited him to sing at a conference. He politely declined, on the grounds that he had retired from his singing career. Still more years later, I invited him to serve on a Traditional Music Committee of Berea College, to help plan a traditional festival and develop a recorded archive of Appalachian music. Bradley readily agreed to serve and is one of the most enthusiastic supporters of Berea College. He not only agreed to sing in the first festival, he donated his songbooks, files of songs and sheet music and a Sears Roebuck Bradley Kincaid guitar to Berea for its library and museum collections. He also gave Berea College the rights to his collected songs.

It seemed to me that Berea College and the wider public should benefit from these gifts to a greater extent than just having them preserved in collections. Also, I thought that Bradley's story should be told—to his many fans who may have lost track of him and also to the many young folk music enthusiasts who never had a chance to hear him sing. This book, therefore, was prepared to tell of Bradley's life and his importance in the American musical scene and also to share some of his songs with those who will appreciate them.

I have enjoyed this work because it gave me an opportunity to get acquainted with Bradley, some of his fans, fellow performers and friends. One is always enriched in the study of the life of another person, and I am grateful for what I have learned from this experience.

I want to thank all of those who helped, starting with John Forbes who perused Bradley's songbooks and compared the music with recordings of Bradley's singing, and who set the tunes on a music typewriter as closely as possible to the way Bradley performed them; and Archie Green, who helped to straighten out publication dates of the songbooks and wrote the introduction. I am indebted to all of those, including Bradley, who granted interviews, wrote letters, furnished information by phone and supplied newsclippings, pictures and songbooks, among whom are: Reuben Powell, John Lair, Scott Wiseman, Norm Cohen, Mattye Belle Kincaid Baker, Don Malin, Jim Ralston, Steve Cisler, Cratis Williams, D. K. Wilgus, George Biggar, Ramona and Marshall "Grandpa" Jones, Joe Troyan, Clarence Anderson, the late Karl Davis, Eddie Nesbitt and Nick Vangoff. I thank Joyce Hancock, Tom Parrish and Janet Kreider for editorial help and Jackie Crowden for help with preparing camera-ready music sheets—also Raymond McLain for musical advice. I acknowledge all of the great help from Genevieve Reynolds who typed the material twice and helped locate all of the pieces of information that I had lost in the piles of Kincaid materials. Finally, I thank the Peer-Southern Organization for permission to include "The Legend of the Robin's Red Breast" on which they own the copyright.

I hope this book will bring back pleasant memories to Bradley's old fans and that it will win new friends for his kind of music.

LOYAL JONES
Berea College
1980

INTRODUCTION

We lack an encompassing history of folksong in the United States, for this body of music—song, singer, style, symbol—has not yet jelled into a unitary mold. Whether we turn to social historian or ethnomusicologist, we do not find an individual who has fashioned a framing device appropriate to the totality of American folksong. Multiple expressions such as Huron war chant, Yankee broadside, Negro spiritual, Delta blues, Blue Ridge frolic, border corrido, and counter-culture complaint may ultimately be pulled together into a single volume, but this is a future task. Sensibly, compilers of popular anthologies and academic scholars have turned to studies of manageable segments of folksong: regional lyrics or their poets, occupational ballads or their heroes, camp meeting hymns or their believers, ethnic songs or their singers.

Biographical studies have proved especially productive in detailing the careers of gifted performers from folk society who, during the 1920s and 1930s, moved to the glowing realm of recording studio, radio station, and publisher's office. In part, we have fine biographies available of figures like Jimmie Rodgers or Bob Wills, because these men attracted fans who eventually surrounded their heroes with lore. But also, the lives of Rodgers and Wills have been compressed into especially strong books because these performers left records, 78-rpm discs as well as printed ephemera. Fortunately, as we face the 1980s, we can anticipate a series of life histories and analytic monographs on many men and women who made the journey from music at the family hearth to music beamed by space satellite.

One such journeyman, Bradley Kincaid, was born in 1895 in

Garrard County, Kentucky, at the Cumberland Mountains' edge, and pioneered by bringing Appalachian folksong to national radio audiences. Also, between 1928 and 1948, he issued a baker's dozen of songbooks which held hundreds of Anglo-American texts and tunes—in effect, a folksong anthology similar to *The American Songbag* compiled by Carl Sandburg. Kincaid ended his active years as a working musician in 1950. For three decades of "retirement," he managed a music store at Springfield, Ohio, returned to the recording scene with a series of retrospective LPs, and shared experiences with inquiring collectors. Loyal Jones, both a folksong enthusiast and careful biographer, interviewed Bradley in the mid-1970s, questioned him about his career, and placed these facts in the sequential study now before us. This modest biography, printed at Kincaid's old school, Berea College, is an affectionate tribute to an appealing musician. More importantly, it becomes a building block in the to-be-written history of American folksong.

Over the years, I have had the pleasure to hear Bradley Kincaid perform, to collect his songbooks, and to interview him. Here, in this preface, I shall not attempt to condense Jones' work; rather, I shall mark a path ahead for readers who wish to focus on conceptual strands within Kincaid's record of achievement.

More than most of his peers, Kincaid understood his personal mediating role between old and new forces contending within the United States during the 1920s. When we examine the careers of other performers who made their way to the radio-recording platform in that era, we find a few who were conscious antiquarians as well as many who revelled in path-breaking tasks. To cite but two: Uncle Dave Macon railed constantly against mechanical and social innovation; Jimmy Rodgers hailed novelty in presentation and delighted in technological affluence. If we accept these artists as polar figures, we must place Kincaid between them.

Does one select deliberately the stance of mediation, or does one simply navigate among the ever-present shoals of reality? At home, Bradley knew the time-tested codes of Southern Highland life; in France during World War I, he used some of the most complex machines then designed for modern times. A few years after war service, he sought opportunity in the city, enrolling during 1924 in Chicago's YMCA College, where he graced its musical quartet. When the Saturday night National Barn Dance surfaced as a popular radio show, the Y quartet made its debut. In time, Bradley appeared alone, turning his familiar "Barbara Allen" into an instantly recognized signature pieces in his repertoire. He responded with a personally edited booklet *Favorite Mountain Ballads and Old Time Songs* (April, 1928).

A year later, for his second booklet, he asked John F. Smith, who taught sociology at Berea, to write an introduction. Smith identified Kincaid's refreshing work as holding songs "direct from the soil" and "close to the heart" in "these days of made-to-order music." Such code words contrasted folksong in its origin and positive meaning with the canned, mechanical, radio-record-disseminated jazz and popular dance music of the period. Professor Smith, a realist, also commended Kincaid for his "effort to preserve some of our choice folksongs in a volume which thousands can afford to purchase." In short, Smith suggested that Chicago's microphones and companion printing presses were suspect in selling "made-to-order music," but were fine tools when they disseminated old treasures from the "rural Southland." Radio—a prime instrument in the relentless modernization of America, a breaker of distance, a lathe shaping national culture—also served urbanites to recall nostalgically their rural birthplace and soil-impacted beliefs.

In six separate printings, Kincaid's first little booklet sold more than 100,000 copies, either by mail order or directly during personal appearances. Each copy served as a tiny bridge linking old and new shores. I see Kincaid as the bridge tender or toll taker, accepting coins from radio fans who needed tangible evidence that old ways had not yet vanished, indeed, that past and present ought to coexist.

Kincaid staked out a position in 1928 which had been conveyed to him during formal years of education, but which troubled other commentators. Kincaid wrote in his first booklet that mountain songs came from "a people in whose veins runs the pure strain of Anglo-Saxon blood. . . ." Careful scholars no longer are impelled to assert either a Teutonic or Elizabethan heritage for Appalachian poetry. We understand that such nineteenth-century formulations were used by Harvard rhetoricians as well as by Kentucky mountain settlement school teachers to give American folksong a blue ribbon pedigree. This emphasis on racial purity paralleled attention to the "superior" patriotic virtue of Anglo-Saxons in the New World. Patriotism and purity formed a banner which waved first over folksong, and eventually over country music.

I touch on one of Kincaid's formulations not to magnify a single element within a complex value system, nor to criticize a now-outmoded position. Professor D. K. Wilgus, the first serious scholar to evaluate Kincaid's contribution, has used the governing label "purist" to place him in relation to his peers. Kincaid carefully distinguished traditional ballads from sentimental parlor songs which had also entered tradition, and both of these early forms from then-recent compositions touching prison life and other marginal experience. In Wilgus' view, the term "purity" covered Kincaid's values as a performing artist in the world of commerce.

To the significance of Kincaid's career choice, I suggest that he was also a teacher in democratic society, consciously using radio and publishing house as a forum for sharing literary/musical gifts with fellow citizens. It is easy for us to look back at Kentucky fans in Chicago who elevated "Barbara Allen" to a symbol of home. However, not all Bradley's listeners were Appalachians stranded in Sandburg's City of the Big Shoulders. Many children of immigrants in steel and the stockyards understood rurality as something distant but precious in their parents' past. I have talked to National Barn Dance enthusiasts who came from the Carpathians, not the Cumberlands, and who sensed no contradiction between their native polkas and exotic banjo breakdowns.

One measure of Kincaid's role is its inner dynamism. He constantly reminded rural listeners of their deep cultural roots, while he also pulled immigrant children out of foreign-language homes into a novel American ambience. Obviously, he relished his prime task; twenty years ago I never thought to ask him how aware, if at all, he was of the second. We lack detailed observations about Appalachian folksong either as a specific tool in the retention of regional or rural ways, or, alternately, as an integrative tool in minority communities. To hear Kincaid's "Barbara Allen" not only as a song about a pair of star-crossed lovers, but also as a figurative survival raft for some and a melting-pot prize for others is a difficult enough assignment for the casual listener. However, such attention to folksong is deeply rewarding.

For readers who wish to use Kincaid's story as a prelude to imaginative judgment about American experience, I offer a note of background to his opening years as a public performer. During the 1920s when Kincaid, "The Kentucky Mountain Boy," first appeared on radio and when he began to sell his booklets, American folksong, white and black, was already a contradictory and controversial phenomenon. Literally, many intellectuals perceived all southern rural expressions, including folksong, as worthless baubles, crude or unformed. By contrast, Vanderbilt agrarians and Chapel Hill regionalists heard mountain music as a sacramental offering. Similarly, jazz-blues was simultaneously denominated as vibrant and indigenous or degenerate and mindless.

In the years of Kincaid's major appeal on the radio, he, unself-consciously, competed for attention in linguistic definition and esthetic choice with men as far apart as H. L. Mencken, Robert Penn Warren, Erskine Caldwell, Carl Van Vechten, and James Weldon Johnson. Each of these seers had something to say about the folk culture bubbling out of the South while Bradley performed in the North on WLS, WLW, KDKA, and WBZ (Chicago, Cincinnati, Pittsburgh, Boston). Kincaid's hold on listeners was enduring, and, seemingly, untouched by pronouncements in the *American Mercury* or *Vanity Fair*. Yet, today, we see Kincaid as one of the best teachers who wrote the word "folksong" on America's national blackboard, and we know that he helped form our understanding of the substance behind the symbol.

Incorporated in Loyal Jones' book is a discography, which

itself stems from the work of dedicated collectors: John Edwards, Gene Earle, Norm Cohen, Harlan Daniel, to name but a few. Any discography can be read as a listening guide, a simple roll of song titles. However, these titles, in the mind's eye, are potentially translatable into visuals, and Bradley's song list is also a photograph album of mountain farms and log cabins, of crossroad hamlets and family parlors. Kincaid collected off the beaten trail, favored a Houn' Dog guitar, and, for photos in some booklets, discarded his early suit-and-tie for a comfortable open-necked checkered shirt. When we use the Kincaid discography for listening today, we are fully conscious that each song represents faded pictures as well as familiar performing styles. Listeners ahead in the 1980s, like those of the past in the 1920s, will know that Bradley Kincaid always invoked quintessential American values.

I have suggested that Kincaid deliberately used bygone themes to cope with the booming reality which he faced in Chicago in the mid-1920s. On the air, he kept listeners closely informed of the growth of his children, placing himself constantly in the center of a model family. In booklets, he credited his wife Irma, a graduate of the Oberlin Conservatory, for arranging music. Not only did he share technical credit by this gesture, but he used it also to reinforce notions of family solidarity. Additionally, in his booklets he included photos of mountain friends, for example, cousin Sam Hurt, fiddler and corncob pipe carver at Paint Lick, Kentucky. Kincaid was one with Sam by ties of kinship and by shared youthful experience, but Bradley did not, like Sam, remain home. Kincaid was formally educated, financially successful, and skilled enough to deal with commercial entrepreneurs throughout his life. As progressive as any character in a Sinclair Lewis novel, Bradley never gave up his inner belief that old folksongs composed a healing balm, good medicine for people uprooted by the harshness of industrial and urban progress.

Where will Bradley Kincaid fit into the large history of American folk music, if and when a single writer emerges to encompass this challenging subject? Will Kincaid merit a chapter, a page, a paragraph, a line, a footnote? We do not know. We cannot answer this rhetorical question because such an overarching volume is not at hand and we can sight but dimly its diverse contours. We are in Loyal Jones' favor for marshalling the facts of Kincaid's life, which will prepare for ultimate evaluation of his role. Meanwhile, readers of this biography can begin to form their particular appreciation.

Bradley Kincaid, in mid-life, sensed something of his position in the American musical scene, and he placed a few lines of self-appraisal on paper. During and after World War II, Bradley had served a stint at the Grand Ole Opry. While offering folksongs at the Ryman Auditorium, he was judged an antiquarian by then-emerging stars of country music. There was no place for Kincaid on the Opry stage when Nashville came to be dominated by men such as Hank Williams, Chet Atkins, and Eddie Arnold. Presciently, Kincaid dedicated his final songbook (1948), to Berea College. There, by good teachers, he had been made conscious of his personal mountain heritage, and of the timeless resonance within American folksong. Hence, his last song folio, printed on pulp paper, became a graduation valedictory for Berea students. Kincaid saw these students both as pure in heart, and as representative of the folk in the mountains who treasured old song.

We know that Berea helped most of its students accommodate to modernity beyond the mountains. But in the process, some graduates tempered modern advance, slowed it down, or, metaphorically, retarded its flame. Kincaid, who helped in this mediating process, never tilted at technological windmills, literal or figurative. He enjoyed to the full the "windmill" interior of radio station and recording studio, and he worked closely with printers, when his own songs flowed from memory to folio page. Seemingly, he never adopted a quixotic stance, nor donned a costume which denigrated mountain life at the altar of urbanity.

Kincaid's musical gifts are obvious to those who search out his initial recordings. The biography before us–dramatic intrinsically and useful to a potential history of folksong–reveals something of his other gifts: facility in teaching outside the classroom, strength to use innovative studio and press to mark continuity from past to present, understanding that folksong is a beacon on modernity's road.

Despite the fact that some antique songs touched dishonor and despair, Kincaid felt that most ballad heroes and heroines were as pure at heart as his companion mountain singers of folksong. Essentially, Kincaid took folksong, a tranquil and beloved gift from childhood, and used high technology to share this tranquillity with millions of listeners. Our very conception today, that much American folksong is by definition undefiled, a precious elixir for national well-being, stems in part from Bradley Kincaid's achievement.

ARCHIE GREEN
University of Texas
1980

PART I

Me oh my, I get high on Bradley Kincaid.
Who, Who, Who, Who is Bradley Kincaid?
*Who, Who, Who, Who is Bradley Kincaid?**

These words are a refrain from a recent song by two young Nashville songwriters. This book is an answer to their question.

Bradley Kincaid, born of poor parents in the foothills of the Kentucky Cumberlands, became one of the first and most popular radio performers in the country. At Station WLS in Chicago, he received more than 100,000 fan letters each year. During his first four weeks at WLW in Cincinnati, 50,000 people wrote to him. His songbooks sold more than 400,000 copies, and on his first personal appearance he found people in queues around the block at the theater where he was to appear. Most of our parents or grandparents knew who he was. Such persons as D. K. Wilgus, Doc Hopkins, Mac Wiseman, Grandpa and Ramona Jones, Scott Wiseman and Bill Monroe have spoken of his influence on them.

What sort of man was Bradley Kincaid, and why was he so popular? Let us see.

"I was born in Garrard County, Kentucky, right at the edge of the Cumberland Mountains, way back at the head of the holler, where the boulevard dwindles down to a squirrel's path and loses itself at the foot of a giant tree," he said.[1] Young Bradley came into the world on July 13, 1895, the fourth of nine children. (Lewis, Viola, Ann, Bradley, Charlie, one baby who died at birth, Mattye Belle, Sadie Katheryn and John.) His

* "Who is Bradley Kincaid?" by Vince Matthews and Glen Sherley. Copyright, 1976 by Peer-Southern Organization.

parents were William Plummer and Elizabeth Hurt Kincaid, both Kentuckians from generations back. His father was a farm laborer whose heart was more in his fox hunting than in farming. Their home was near the Point Leavell community, 18 miles from Berea on the pike between Lancaster and Paint Lick. The house they lived in was a former storehouse on the property of Bradley's Grandfather Hurt. When Elizabeth and William married, they clapboarded the log structure, added a lean-to and fixed up the roof. Grandfather Hurt's long two-story house, with huge chimneys at either end, had only recently been upgraded from a log house to a clapboard house.

Bradley grew up in the eastern third of Kentucky just at the edge of the mountains. Garrard County is an area of rolling hills, mostly cleared for cultivation or pasture. To the east is Madison County whose south-eastern portion sweeps up into the Cumberlands. To the north is Jessamine County, separated from Garrard by the Kentucky River, crowded by bluffs and knobs. Lincoln County, with more hills, lies to the south, and Boyle and the Bluegrass are to the west. In Bradley's youth, it was a land of farmers. Coal and factories were miles away. Sheep and cattle, tobacco and corn were the main products. The latter two required a good deal of manual labor, and Bradley's father, and later his children, hired out as workers on nearby farms. The farms were better than the steep acres in the nearby Cumberland Mountains, but they were not nearly so good as those in the lush Bluegrass region. Much of the soil was a thin layer over limestone and shale, and its moisture yielded quickly to frequent dry spells. Most people worked hard to make a living, and a living was all that most had to show for their labor.

The people were descended, for the most part, from English and Scotch-Irish settlers, with the former being more numerous in eastern Kentucky. Names of Scottish origin, such as Kincaid, Duncan and McQuerry were common in Garrard County. The people came from independent and traditional folk who had tried to escape bad government, oppressive religion or hard times. They had brought with them the British ballads and folk songs, Old World tales and riddles, Calvinist religion and values, old-fashioned customs and superstitions. Along the way in their journey from the Chesapeake or the Carolina coast, through the mountains of Virginia and North Carolina, Tennessee and the Cumberland Gap, they had been joined by Germans and a few French, and their customs commingled. Some had married with and all had learned from the Cherokees. Thus they were not the same as their forebears who had first landed on American shores, but they were still independent and traditional. They had held on to much from the past, especially that which was their bag of tricks—with which they entertained, inspired and lulled their children, and themselves. The long trek had put schools behind them, and their widely-scattered settlement patterns did not encourage adequate schools, so that a generation or two may have skipped formal learning altogether.

It was mostly an oral society. There was the Bible and sometimes copies of the classics, but for the most part, frontier people were not readers. This did not mean, however, that they did not have a literature or a legacy of beliefs, skills and practical knowledge. This literature resided in the memories of the people. There was specialization, to be sure, and not everyone was adept at learning that which was needed. In a community, one might be the ballad singer, another the fiddler or banjo picker, another the teller of tales, the blacksmith, chimney builder, interpreter of religion, and so on. Yet they shared a way of life, and most held the same beliefs and assumptions about the human condition, and each knew some of the vast heritage that they jointly possessed and daily put to use.

Much of the music was unaccompanied by instruments, sung out while the singer worked at churn or plow. The old tragic ballads and love songs were often sung when the heart was heavy with personal sorrow or grief. The impersonal tragedy of the ballads served as a means of confronting and throwing off one's own melancholia. All, children and adults alike, were fascinated by the intricate, yet readily understandable plots of the ballads and tales. Each young lover could resonate to the lyric love songs and laments of unrequited lovers of long ago. This literature bound the people to the past generations and their experiences. It is the warp and woof of culture.

Although usually the music-making was a solitary offering out of the personal feelings of the singer, much of the traditional lore happened at communal gatherings that were common in earlier times—house raisings, corn shuckings, bean stringings, candy pullings, or perhaps just a party at which some might fiddle or pick while others danced to the distinctive Appalachian square dance, and one might sing or charm everyone with quiet dilcimer music. Others would tell tales, perhaps from local experiences or else based on the Old World tales and legends.

Religion sometimes separated the dancers and lovers of secular music from those who confined their singing to the church. Both groups persisted, and there was frequent crossing over the lines, so that most people were familiar with the hymns of the various churches as well as the secular string music and songs. Of course, not all of the churches segregated things so neatly, and some did not see a problem with secular music, or even dancing, as long as it was separate from the doctrine and music in the church service. Rural religious people everywhere are usually traditional people, and so were the rural Kentuckians among whom Bradley Kincaid grew up. The culture was rich in traditional arts, and one who was interested could learn a plenty.

Both Elizabeth and William Kincaid were singers, and it was from them that Bradley learned his first songs.

> My father was quite a singer. He led singing in church and Sunday School. We were Campbellites or Christian Church. I remember him very well getting ahold of a piece of music. He had one of these tuning forks. He'd hit that against something and get the tone, "Do, me, so, do, so me do"—get the pitch and off he'd go, reading those notes. A good many of the books had shape notes, and he could read those very well. That was my introduction to music, and all through the years I could remember hearing my father singing songs like "Two Little Girls in Blue," "After the Ball," "Kitty Wells" and songs like that.
>
> But my mother, she went further back. She sang the old

> English ballads. I learned a lot of ballads from her, like "Fair Ellender," "The Two Sisters" and any number of English ballads. I sang these as a kid. I didn't sing so much in church. Course I sang in Sunday School class, but I didn't do solos or anything like that. My mother never did show too much musical ability, though she used to—in a very lamentable voice—sing some of the old blood curdlers to me, and my hair would stand straight up on my head.[2]

His repertory of songs, then, began building early and naturally, entirely in the oral tradition. He commented to a reporter years later that he had picked up more than eighty songs while he lived in the Kentucky hills.[3]

Mountain people have always been known as traders, a skill usually brought on by necessity. When no money was available, it was necessary to barter what you had for whatever you wanted. An important trade took place when Bradley was a young boy.

> We lived in that country where there was a lot of fox hunting. Well, my father used to go out with some of the fox hunters, and they'd take their dogs and get on top of some ridge and set the dogs off down in the hollow chasing a fox. They'd build up a fire and sit around and talk and tell stories. And on one of these occasions, a Negro friend of my father's, who would fox-hunt with them once in a while, had this guitar, and my father traded him one of the fox hounds for the guitar. And he brought it home, and all of the kids learned to play it.[4]

Guitars at the time were much rarer than fox hounds. They had started to nudge out the traditional banjo, fiddle and dulcimer early in the twentieth century, thanks to travelers and the mail-order houses. The guitar that William Kincaid brought home the morning after the fox hunt was one of unknown make, identified only with the code 37/BLL. It was small by today's standards. Bradley learned to play it on long summer evenings, when the work was done and he would tilt a chair back against the wall and pick and sing for hours. He was to keep the little guitar throughout his career (although he later performed with a Gibson and a fancier 1929 Martin 000-45) and relinquished it only to the Country Music Hall of Fame.

Bradley grew up working, hiring himself out to local farmers. His first job was riding a corn planter for twenty-five cents a day. He later got fifty cents and then seventy-five. "When I made a dollar a day," he said, "I thought I had arrived. That was good money in that day."

He attended Back Creek School, which met three months each year. The schoolhouse was a converted log cabin about two miles from the Kincaids' home. "The teacher was usually an eighth grade graduate who could get a license to teach school," he remembered. "I went through the fifth grade, and then I was out of school. My mother died about that time, and I was on my own from then on."

Although he talks very little about these years, life was hard for him. His father remarried fairly soon and moved to Stanford, Kentucky, taking with him only the two youngest children, Mattye Belle and Katheryn. The rest remained at the old home place. Except for some guidance from his older sister Viola and her husband Mike Burnside, Bradley was on his own at the age of thirteen. Naturally enough, the break-up of the family had a profound effect on him, creating a great insecurity in his childhood years and leaving him with a feeling of unworthiness. His father was indifferent toward the older children. (It was not until many years later, when he was a successful entertainer, that Bradley moved toward a reconciliation by buying a farm for his father in Ohio.) For a time Bradley worked on farms in Garrard County, and then when he was fourteen he went to Louisville and got a job in a wheel factory, making ten cents an hour. After two years, however, he came back to Garrard County.

> I just didn't see any hope for Bradley Kincaid because I had no education, and I was working on the farm for a dollar a day. My brother-in-law and I decided to raise a crop of tobacco. We rented eight acres on the halves. We worked all summer raising that tobacco. We had 11,400 pounds. I remember it just as well, and we got about ten cents a pound for it. I had worked all year, and when we figured it up, I got about forty dollars for my year's work. I decided to shake the dust of the

place off my feet.[5]

But something significant happened to Bradley Kincaid, which he talks about hesitantly, as if he were afraid he might be misunderstood.

About that time we were having an old-fashioned revival meeting, where the preacher came for two weeks and preached these emotional sermons. I was going to the meetings every night at Point Leavell Fairview Christian Church, and I was rather cynical about it. I wasn't too strong on religion in those days. Of course I went to church because that was a social place. That was the only place where you ever met anybody in the country, back in a remote place like we were. There were no social gatherings except for dances in the winter. Generally, there was no social life except in the church, and so I went to those meetings.

It so happened that a friend of mine of long standing, a boy who has been very successful over the years—he was from down there at Paint Lick—Jim Ralston. He became a successful businessman in the Ralston-Purina organization. He was just a young fellow then—about my own age, and he took me aside one night and said, "Bradley, you ought to join the church. You've fooled around long enough. It's time you were changing things." He talked me into "going forward" that night. So I went forward and something—sort of a change—came over me, and for several days I wondered what this was all about. I got a feeling that I wanted to improve myself. I'm not giving this too much emphasis, but something happened to Bradley Kincaid, and I began to see the light a little bit and that I could get away from following a pair of "hard-tails"—as we called a pair of mules—around a forty-acre field all day with a No. 40 plow.[6]

James Ralston, now of Phoenix, Arizona, retired from Ralston-Purina Company and a vigorous eighty-two when he was interviewed, remembered that night in almost the same way.

Bradley and I liked to double-date. He was rambling around the country, but he was likeable, a wonderful personality. I had a cousin who lived down at Point Leavell, and we'd go down there on week-ends—spend Saturday night with her and her husband. We went to church this particular night—Point Leavell Christian Church; it's still there, about halfway between Paint Lick and Lancaster. At that time I was interested in church work. We'd never talked about church, but I said to Bradley, "I think you ought to go up there and declare yourself." He got up and went forward. It amazed me, because I didn't expect to see any results like that, but Bradley took it very seriously. In a very short time I found out he had decided to go back to school and make something of himself. He made a change in his life right then. He came to Berea and started to school.[7]

Berea College was only seventeen miles from the Kincaid home, and Bradley and his family had been there many times to commencement programs, which were very popular social events, drawing hundreds of people from the surrounding territory. At the time Berea had several divisions: an academy, a foundation high school, a normal school and a college. It also had an ungraded section and encouraged mountain young people to come with whatever level of education they might have and start from there. "Somehow I got to thinking about Berea. I came to Berea in the fall of 1914. I had just had a few years of a three-month school. I had finished McGuffey's old Fifth Grade Reader, which was as far as I could go in my school at home. So at the age of nineteen, I came to Berea. I'll tell you the cows licked through the fence at me I was so green."[8] He had then been out of school for ten years.

I entered the sixth grade. I got a job waiting tables and odd jobs. I think they paid ten cents an hour then. After a while I got a job as head waiter at Ladies Hall, and I got a dollar and a half a week for that. I was paying a dollar thirty-five for board and sixty cents a week for a room. I found it very easy to make my way. I began to get my eyes and ears open.

I came in contact with that wonderful, wonderful Dean [Thomas A.] Edwards, who was one of the finest men Berea ever had. He knew grammar—English—like nobody else I've ever seen. He was the man who opened my eyes to the fact that Bradley Kincaid could be something. Up until that time, I was afraid to express myself because I had sense enough to know that I didn't understand English very well, and that I could make many mistakes. So I kept my mouth shut. He kind of opened my mouth. That was the beginning of me.

I remember how timid I was about going into that first class, because I was almost six feet tall and going in with little sixth graders. But when I got inside, I soon was calmed down because there was a big fellow across the aisle from me who must have been six feet two, and he was twenty-three years old—came from way up in West Virginia.

Professor Ralph Rigby, John F. Smith and Gladys Jameson had influence on me. Miss Jameson—oh, she was wonderful. She was the first one that led me to believe that I could sing. She used to give me lessons—no fee for it or anything. She'd get me off to a piano and run notes, "See if you can go up here." I'd hit a high note, and she'd just beam. I could reach high D flat.

There are more names than I can think of, of people who were wonderful to me—H. E. Taylor. He gave me a job at Boone Tavern (the college hotel) at fifty dollars a month and my room and board. I had to get up at night to answer the bell. Taylor gave me a job as his secretary—to do stenographic work. I used to take letters on one of the first talking machines. Professor John Smith collected ballads and I helped him.[9]

After Bradley got the job at Boone Tavern, he helped his younger sisters Mattye Belle and Katheryn enroll at Berea, and he and an older sister, Ann, helped them financially while they were in school.

Bradley finished the sixth, seventh and eighth grades in two years. By then the First World War was in full swing, and so he and his old friend Jim Ralston joined the army.

Ralston remembered the early months of their service.

I went in the first draft to Camp Taylor in Louisville. Very shortly thereafter, Bradley came down—and how we got in the

> same company, I don't know. We worked it out somehow, and we had bunks together. We were there for almost a year. We'd get week-end passes and go down to the Broadway Baptist Church. We'd go to Sunday School and the young people's meeting. We had a great time dating girls together. We met a lot of nice people. You know how they treat servicemen.
>
> I was transferred to Atlanta, Georgia, and Bradley was sent somewhere else. We corresponded. Every once in a while I got a letter telling about some beautiful girl he'd met.[10]

Bradley spent two years in service, one of them in France with the Eighty-fourth Division. Ralston was discharged from the army earlier than Bradley and became a salesman for Storrs-Schaefer Tailoring Company in Cincinnati. He begged Bradley to join the company also, after his discharge. This Bradley did, but he quit after a few months and returned to Berea. "This decision," Ralston wrote, "I am sure, was a demonstration of Bradley's determination to be something more than a traveling salesman or average person." [11] He enrolled in the Berea Academy and finished in three years. "That doesn't mean I was particularly smart at all," Bradley said wryly, "but after all I had knocked around. I'd gone to Louisville, 125 miles away and worked in a wheel shop . . . so, I'd had worldly experience. Naturally, I got along a little faster than the students who were the right ages to be in the classes." [12]

Bradley never missed a chance to praise Berea College as his intellectual birthplace. He devoted pages in his early songbooks to Berea and told of what it meant to him.

> Had it not been for the advantages Berea College offers to mountain boys and girls I probably would never have received any education . . .[13]
>
> I was one of those who started in the sixth grade at the age of nineteen, and through the help and encouragement of Berea was able eventually to secure a college degree. I am proud of that. Not because of an academic standing, but because, after spending nineteen years in darkness and ignorance, Berea helped me to see the light. I owe it all to her—a debt I can never pay, but I hereby gratefully acknowledge it.[14]

Bradley was twenty-six when he graduated from the Berea Academy. A high school certificate was not all he got at Berea. He fell in love with his music teacher, Irma Foreman, or as he put it, "Cupid came along and interfered with my progress. So I got married."[15] Irma Foreman was a native of Brooklyn, but she had moved to Oberlin, Ohio, with her family after the death of her father, so that she and the other children might get an education at Oberlin College. The person who had encouraged them to move to Oberlin was their pastor in Brooklyn, Dr. William J. Hutchins, who later became president of Berea College. When Irma graduated from the Oberlin Conservatory of Music, Hutchins invited her to come to Berea to teach.[16]

Bradley and Irma were married in 1922, and he went to work for the YMCA in Kentucky, as a district secretary, stationed at Lebanon. Then one day, about two years later, Irma said to him, "I see that you would like to have a college education." She knew that it bothered him somewhat that she was a college graduate and he wasn't. So, after talking it over, they sold most of their belongings for "the munificent sum of $412" and caught the train for Chicago. There Bradley enrolled in the YMCA College, later to be renamed George Williams College. Irma worked as a telephone switchboard operator until she was able to get a better job as women's activities director at the La Porte, Indiana, YMCA, some sixty miles from Chicago, where Bradley also worked part-time later on. Bradley eventually became a member of the YMCA quartet which sang at luncheon clubs, conventions and the like, traveling as far away as Milwaukee. Thus they made enough money to live on while Bradley studied.[17]

The quartet eventually took him to Radio Station WLS, which was owned by the Sears-Roebuck Agricultural Foundation and had been on the air since April of 1924. By 1926, the station had developed a variety in the kinds of music it presented, but the most popular program of all was the National Barn Dance which had shocked officials of the Sears organization when it went on the air from the Sherman Hotel on April 19, 1924 with a fiddle band, cowbells and a great deal of ungenteel enthusiasm. It was an instant hit, and thus reservations of the Sears bigwigs were set aside. Since the Barn Dance emphasized rural music, the manager of the quartet, knowing that Bradley knew many folk songs, insisted that he tell Don Malin, the musical director of the station, about them. He came, "rather diffidently," as Malin put it, and told him how he had learned such ballads as "Barbara Allen" and "Fair Ellender" from his mother. "I was brought up on them," he said.

"Well, how would you like to come down and sing a few of them on the Barn Dance on Saturday night?" Malin asked.[18] Bradley admits that at the time he wasn't too much interested in singing ballads because he had been taking voice lessons and studying semi-classical music. But he also knew that he needed to make a living, and so he agreed to perform, after he learned that he would be paid fifteen dollars. He had not brought his guitar to Chicago with him. In fact, he had not played it recently. He found a student at the college dormitory who owned one, and he borrowed it in time to practice a few chords.

"I went down there and sang "Barbara Allen" and a few of the other old-timers for them," Bradley remembers. "And they were so impressed that they asked me to be on their regular staff for fifteen dollars every Saturday night. Well, for a college student that only had donuts and coffee for breakfast, that was pretty good."

The main reason the station managers were impressed was the mail response to Bradley. The mail impressed Bradley also.

> So in the course of time, I got interested in it a little more. Here was the clincher. One day after I'd been singing there for three or four weeks, I went down one Saturday afternoon a little early, and the girl at the outer desk said, 'Bradley, there's some mail back there in the back room for you.' Well, it'd never occurred to me that anyone would ever write and say anything about Bradley Kincaid. I went back there. You've seen these big laundry baskets about the size of a desk. Here was this basket full of fan mail. I took all I could carry home with me, and everywhere I read where they said, "You're the best singer on the air," I believed them.[19]

The last sentence was meant as a joke. Actually, he had doubted that many people would be interested in the old songs or in him as a singer. It took the mail response to convince him that he was appreciated. He received more than 300,000 fan letters while he was at WLS and became the first big radio star in the United States. There was something about his unaffected manner, his modest and simple style, his clear and sweet tenor voice and the old songs he sang that made him an instant success. His fans didn't just like him, they adored him and they depended on him. They never tired of hearing "Barbara Allen" and the other old ballads that he presented.

Clockwise from top: Bradley as infant, student at Berea, World War I soldier and college student in Chicago.

II

Without being aware of it, Bradley Kincaid had stumbled into commercial music in its time of greatest need. Records and radio were becoming popular, and executives of the industries had discovered that there was a rural population and city folk with rural roots who were eager for rural music. Yet, there were not many talented folk and country artists who had been "discovered" or who had presented themselves for auditions. Record companies were still trying to figure out what kind of music would sell, and radio executives were slowly varying their programs from simi-classical and popular music to include folk and what was to become country music.

Phonograph recordings developed commercially a long time before radio did. Edison invented his recording device in 1877 and some cylinder recordings were on the market before the turn of the century, but until the early twenties, recordings were almost exclusively of classical, semi-classical and popular (parlor and sentimental) music. The potential of recordings was enhanced greatly by the development of disc-type recorders in 1921. At that time Ralph Peer, working for Okeh Records and who was later to be associated with Bradley, became aware that many black people had moved to the cities, had gotton jobs and were a good potential market for music that they liked. In 1920, Peer had recorded Mamie Smith, whose records were in much demand. He went forth looking for more black talent, and in the course of his search he also found talented white musicians. Aside from Peer's work, however, some white musicians sought out record companies, feeling that their talents were worthy of the record market. Two were Eck Robertson, a flashy Texas fiddler, and a Virginia champion fiddler, Henry Gilliland, who met at a Virginia Civil War reunion in 1922 and decided to go to Victor studios in New York to be recorded. They were followed the next year by Henry Whitter of Virginia to record "The Wreck on the Southern Old 97" for Victor.[20]

But the first recordings that really started the trend toward folk-country music were those of Fiddlin' John Carson of Georgia by Ralph Peer for Okeh in June of 1923.[21] The way this came about tells something of the problems rural musicians faced with recording executives. Polk Brockman, whose father ran a furniture store in Atlanta which also carried a line of phonograph records, talked Ralph Peer into recording Carson, a fiddler-singer, house painter and reputed one-time moonshiner. Peer did not like Carson's singing and was reluctant to issue a record. However, Brockman ordered 500 copies to sell in the store, and Peer agreed to produce them. These were soon sold and more ordered. Only then did Peer give the record a number and place it in the Okeh catalogue. He then put Carson under contract to Okeh to record more numbers in their New York studios.[22]

The success of the early folk-country records inspired record companies to set up temporary studios in several southern cities and musicians to seek them out. During 1924, several others became recording artists: Gid Tanner and Riley Puckett from Georgia; Samantha Bumgarner, whom Bascom Lamar Lunsford called the most complete music-maker he knew, and Eva Davis from western North Carolina; and Ernest "Pop" Stoneman and his Dixie Mountaineers from Virginia. The next year Al and Joe Hopkins took a string band to Okeh studios in New York City. When asked the name of the band, they replied that they were "just a bunch of Hillbillies," so Okeh listed them as the "Hillbillies."[23] The term "hillbilly" came to be associated with the range of rural music of the day, just as "race" was applied to the recorded music of and for black people. Several of the recording companies designated certain labels for music that they variously called "hillbilly," "hill country tunes," "old-time music," or "old familiar tunes." Folk-country music became big business.[24]

Bradley Kincaid was one of several performers who objected strongly to the word "hillbilly" connected with the music he presented. A man of education, he appreciated the origin and quality of his music, and he resented its being belittled by the term. He was well aware, no doubt, of the contempt with which some people viewed folk and country music, and he argued that it was authentic British and American folk music, as distinctive as the Negro spirituals. Some of the western musicians made the most of their cowboy clothing to offset the "hillbilly" image.[25] Other musicians minded the designation not at all.

The success of old-time music caused several record companies to engage talent scouts in various parts of the South. Ralph Peer was the best-known, working for Okeh and later Victor, because it was he who recorded Jimmie Rodgers and the Carter Family in 1927 in Bristol, Tennessee-Virginia. But there were others such as the afore-mentioned Polk C. Brockman who scouted in Atlanta and other places like Asheville where he recorded fifty-eight sides; and Dennis Taylor of Richmond, Kentucky, who delivered Dock Roberts, Edgar Boaz, Marion Underwood, Jim Booker and Welby Toomey to Gennett Studios in Richmond, Indiana, but who turned down a young man called Red Foley because he did not like his singing.[26]

Jimmie Rodgers became the first big country recording star. During his short six years of recording, he sold twenty million records. But others also did well, such as the Carter Family, the Georgia Skillet Lickers, as well as Bradley Kincaid, who began recording in 1927. The phonograph record business had grown to total sales of 104 million by 1927. Sales slipped to a mere six million in the first year of the Depression and with the growing popularity of radio, but old-time music continued to sell.[27]

Radio did not become a commercial possibility until 1920, even though Marconi had invented the wireless in 1895. KDKA in Pittsburg and KNX in Los Angeles were two of the first stations to start broadcasting. By 1924 there were approximately 600 stations in the United States.[28]

The early receiving sets were without speakers, and headphones had to be used. But radio became very popular, and after external speakers were developed, it was possible to get better sound over radio than from mechanically amplified phonographs. The early stations were set up, for the most part, by newspapers or other businesses as a public service. Sears-Roebuck started WLS. The National Life and Accident Insurance Company started WSM in Nashville. They did not advertise but rather expected good will to accrue to the owners. The early musicians were not paid but were happy at a chance to play over the new invention. Records could not be used because of their poor reproduction, and thus it was necessary for the stations to find musicians for their programs.[29]

The first radio station to produce a show aimed at rural audiences was WBAP, Fort Worth. At first they had used only pop, jazz and semi-classical music, the pattern of other stations. Then on January 4, 1923, they created a one-and-a-half hour square dance program directed by ex-Confederate Captain M. J. Bonner, and his string band. WBAP was heard over much of the country, and this program inspired other barn dance shows.[30]

The Sears-Roebuck Agricultural Foundation obtained a license to start a radio station in Chicago in 1923 for the purpose of helping farmers with crop and weather reports. This station became WLS (World's Largest Store) with a dedication program on April 12, 1924. Ethel Barrymore, the great dramatic actress, and William S. Hart, the silent screen cowboy, were among those on the program. Miss Barrymore took one look at the microphone and froze. One observer claimed that she fainted away. Whereupon, William S. Hart stepped forward and read "Invictus" by William Ernest Henley.[31]

WLS set out to be a farmer's station, in contrast to other stations that catered to the assumed interests of city dwellers. Most of the other Chicago stations played grand opera and classical or semi-classical music. WLS gave weather and market reports, homemaker hints, but it did have a staff organist (Ralph Waldo Emerson) and other conventional entertainers and musicians. However, within the week, it inaugurated a Barn Dance (April 19, 1924) which grew into the most popular such show in the country for a time and was one of the longest-running continuous shows ever. The first music was from Tommy Dandurand's fiddle band, augmented with cowbells.[32] It said that Sears officials were outraged at the rural sound and its unfettered boistrousness, but the mail rolled in and assured its future.

The station soon moved its studios to where there was room for a small audience. Then, it eventually took over the Eighth Street Theatre to accommodate the crowds which shortly filled the theatre for two shows each Saturday night.

WLS soon hired George D. Hay, known as the Solemn Old Judge, away from WMC, Memphis. He was an old newspaperman, who reported that he had gone to the Ozarks to cover a war hero's funeral, had been invited to a hoedown and had there gotten the idea for a country barn dance show.[33] However, it appears that credit for originating the show should go to Edgar Bill, program director at WLS. It is said that he called the staff together and suggested an old country dance type program. Besides Dandurand's band they got Tom Owen, through an announcement over the air, to call square dances. The first musicians included Ford and Glenn, Grace Wilson and Chubby Parker. None was paid, but one of Al Capone's girlfriends, so a tale goes, later played on the show and the gangster strongly urged that she be paid, and she was. Others asked for equal treatment.[34]

Nashville's WSM Grand Ole Opry, the next big country music show, was started on November 28, 1925, by George D. Hay, who was hired as the first station director at WSM and who became the chief Opry announcer. The first night's show consisted of Uncle Jimmy Thompson playing fiddle, with his niece, Eva Thompson Jones, playing piano accompaniment. They had a favorable response, and this pair continued to play alone for several weeks until other musicians volunteered, just for their own enjoyment. Eventually, several bands joined up, such as Dr. Humphrey Bate's Possum Hunters, the Crook Brothers, the Gully Jumpers, the Fruit Jar Drinkers and Sam and Kirk McGee.[35]

Later, other country music shows were started: Renfro Valley Barn Dance, the WWVA Jamboree (Wheeling), the Louisiana Hayride, and so on. They were all popular. The National Barn Dance had two million people pay to see its shows between 1932 and 1950.[36] Both the National Barn Dance and Grand Ole Opry have had a vast radio audience.

Radio caught on fast. Sales of sets went from $60,000 in

1922 to $842,248,000 in 1929. By 1930, 12,074,345 homes were equipped.[37] It was customary for those with radios to invite those without for an evening of listening to favorite shows. Thus a great portion of the population was oriented toward radio by the end of the twenties.

Most of the early recording and radio performers on the folk-country shows had to rely on material that they already knew: traditional ballads and songs, sentimental parlor songs that had gotten into the oral tradition, hymns, fiddle tunes and the like. These, or songs of similar motif or sentiment, were the music that a great part of their audiences had listened to all of their lives. It was a music of the heart and emotions, close to folk traditions and values. As an indication of how folk-oriented the early music was, folklorist D. K. Wilgus estimates that one-third of the songs in any folk collection in the South have been recorded on hillbilly records.[38] Soon, of course, arrangers and composers set to work to produce variations or entirely new material based on the tried-and-true folk themes. And country music was on its way.

Bradley Kincaid was the first artist to become a radio star using almost entirely authentic folk music, although there were many others from his part of the country who also made good in recordings or radio. They included the Grand Ole Opry's Uncle Dave Macon, Doc Hopkins, the Rev. Buell Kazee, Asa Martin, Dock Boggs, the Carter Family, Asher and Jimmy Sizemore, Ernest Stoneman, the Stanley Brothers and a host of others. They filled a need created by the recording and broadcasting industries.

III

Bradley became known as The Kentucky Mountain Boy. "They thought I was going to be popular," he said, "and they wanted to get a catchy name. They said, 'How'd you get started in this?' And I told them about my father trading a foxhound for the guitar. They said, 'That's it, Bradley Kincaid and his Houn' Dog guitar.' "[39]

He wasn't just a singer. Managers of the station, which Sears-Roebuck later sold to *The Prairie Farmer* magazine, saw how well he related to rural people and hired him also as an announcer, after he had graduated from college. Some of his fans became alarmed that this new job might keep him from singing to them. The station manager, therefore, encouraged him to sing as a part of his Dinner Bell program at noon, and he continued to sing on the Barn Dance. In addition, he also ran a radio club for teenagers, called the Twelve and Twenty Club, which stressed character and personality development. He occasionally wrote inspirational pieces for *The Prairie Farmer* and other publications. Thus his Berea and YMCA training was put to good use. As an announcer, Bradley gave farmers the most up-to-date and helpful information that could be gathered on markets, weather, new techniques in farming, and the like.

The station at the time was run entirely as a public service. Its managers prided themselves on being able to answer any questions or requests that came in. Therefore, when people began writing in for the words and music to some of the old songs that Bradley sang, the manager, Edgar Bill, approached Bradley about putting out a songbook. Bradley doubted that there would be many people who would want to buy a book of the old songs.

> Well, in order to please him, I sat down at the typewriter and wrote out about twenty-two of these songs that I knew

> from memory, and my wife, as I hummed the tunes for her, she wrote down the melody notes . . . . I took them down and laid them on Mr. Bill's desk. He said, "No, you get them fixed up, get a printer in here and get them to publish them. Maybe you can sell them for fifty cents and get your expenses back." I said all right. So we brought in a printer, and we made arrangements. He said, "How many do you think you ought to get published first?" I said, "Oh, a couple of thousand, anyway." So, a couple of days before the songbooks came off the press, I announced a couple of times on the air that I had a little songbook if they'd like to have one–if they'd send fifty cents to me at the station . . . . Two days later we had more than 10,000 orders. I called the printer . . . . and told him to print another 10,000. He said, "Why not 20,000?" I said yes. So then we got to printing in 50,000 lots.[40]

His first book was entitled *My Favorite Mountain Ballads and Old-Time Songs*. It went through six printings, the first in April of 1928 and the sixth in July of 1929. In a letter "To my Radio Friends," in his second book, *Favorite Old-Time Songs and Mountain Ballads*, published in 1929, he wrote that "more than a hundred thousand letters have reached my desk since my first songbook was published a year ago." In 1930 he published a third book. From comments he made, it appears that he sold around 110,000 of the first book. He commented in his third that "more than two hundred thousand copies of my first two songbooks have been sent out to enthusiastic listeners." He was the first radio entertainer to publish a songbook. Perhaps this is why the managers at WLS took little interest in it. But it was not long until they saw the money coming in. Edgar Bill asked Bradley: "Don't you think we ought to get in on that? How about letting the station publish these?" Bradley agreed to split the profit fifty-fifty.[41]

George Biggar, who was farm and market editor at WLS in 1924 and later program director, had this to say about Bradley's popularity:

> Mrs. Biggar and I recall hearing Bradley Kincaid first on the National Barn Dance in 1926. We knew nothing about him but were impressed by his voice and the songs that he was singing,

most of which were unfamiliar to us. I would say that Bradley introduced to the great Midwest many old English and Appalachian mountain serious "story" songs, as well as lighter traditional melodies, unknown to the vast majority of rural and urban listeners. They became enamored with them in a short time.

It was Bradley's warm, friendly tenor voice with very good diction that was greatly responsible for popularizing these colorful, melodious and "folksy" traditional songs. Bradley's appealing voice, unaccompanied by anything except his own guitar, made his "story" songs really "come to life."

Showmanship employed in building Bradley Kincaid to great acceptance was a big factor in his exceptional popularity on WLS. Musical Director Don Malin scheduled him during periods with greatest audience potential. He booked him for fifteen minute periods "across the board" daytimes, when possible.

On WLS National Barn Dance, Master of Ceremonies Harold Safford saw to it that there was a hush in the program—then Bradley's sweet tenor voice would come in with:

In the hills of old Kentucky
Where the birds sing merrily . . . .

After his short theme—a real attention-getter in listening homes, Harold would introduce the singer in a manner similar to this, "Yes, it's time for a visit with your favorite singer of folk and mountain ballads—Bradley Kincaid, the Kentucky Boy with his Houn' Dog Guitar . . . ." Bradley would then introduce his own numbers, often in dialog with Harold Safford. The program would close with a fade-out of Bradley's theme.

This artist's fan mail was great—and he studied it carefully to build his programs around the numbers most favorably received and consequently requested.[42]

Early radio spawned a new demand in entertainment—the personal appearance. When radio first became a popular entertainment medium, vaudeville declined. People stayed home to listen to radio. Soon, however, they grew curious about the new radio stars and naturally had a desire to see them in person. The WLS team of Ford and Glenn started personal appearances in 1924. Former WLS staffer Clementine Legg Segal wrote that their successful shows caused the station to form the WLS Artists Bureau, with which she became associated:

> Then in the mid-1920s, radio shows were booked into theatres to supplement the generally mediocre silent motion pictures being shown . . . . Bradley Kincaid's addition to the staff of WLS in 1926, his rapid growth in popularity with his appealing tenor rendition of the simple Appalachian folk songs soon created a demand for his personal appearance, not only in theatres near Chicago, but also in rural school auditoriums.[43]

Bradley recalls a surge of new popularity after he had been singing for a while and after his first songbook proved so much in demand:

> The bookers started calling on me. Well, I'd never made a public appearance in my life. They wanted me to go on stage. I said, "Gee whiz, who'd want to see me on the stage." "Well, just let me book you in a couple of theatres and I'll show you." "What would I do?" I said. "Well, you can think up a couple of jokes to tell and sing four or five songs." So I said, "All right."[44]

The town Bradley finally agreed to play was Peoria, Illinois. "When I walked up to the theatre, there was a line several blocks long and people were being turned away. I walked across the street and asked a fellow what was going on. He said, 'Why, that radio singer from WLS is going to be here.' " He mentioned that he had approached that first personal appearance with "fear and trembling" but everything went well and he got either $300 or $400 for appearing.[45]

Getting up on a stage in front of a theatre full of people was not an easy thing for Bradley to do. It went against his modest self-effacing ways, and he was very uncomfortable. Marshall "Grandpa" Jones, who later played with Bradley, reported,

> He told me that the first time he went on—or the first year—he'd stand in one place, afraid to move his feet. His feet would just get numb. Bradley never was, on the stage, a jumping-around fellow. He'd always stand and pick his guitar just as easy and do all of his stuff right in one spot.[46]

In spite of his discomfort, Grandpa Jones remembered that Bradley always enjoyed the people who wanted his autograph. Jones related that while they were playing together, "he'd be mobbed every day with them, wanting his autograph and things like that."[47]

It took him a long time to believe that this many people would come out to see him. He commented that the theatre managers were reluctant to book someone they had never heard of.

> Well, the booker would say, "How much do you do on an average day?" "Well, a couple of hundred dollars." He'd say, "Well, you take the first two hundred, and we'll take the next two hundred and we'll split any over that." So, he couldn't lose that way. He'd book it that way and maybe we'd do anywhere from $600 to $800 in a day . . . . In addition, I'd take along the songbooks and sell hundreds at the door.[48]

Since times were hard, some people did not have the money to pay admission to the shows. "People would come backstage and want to shake hands with me and tell me that they listened to me on the radio and that they just wanted me to know that they knew I was in town but they just didn't have a quarter or fifty cents to go to the show." This observation revealed the personal feeling that Bradley Kincaid inspired in his audience. He became a close and important member of their circle of acquaintances. Clementine Segal commented that WLS tried to be very personal in its relationship with its audience, and Bradley was one of its most personable performers.

> Mr. Edgar L. Bill, WLS Managing Director, always insisted that WLS artists project a handshake and a smile on the air and on their personal appearances. Bradley's warmth and friendliness on the National Barn Dance and his other radio programs were projected to his theatre audiences whenever he

appeared. After holding many audiences past the customary half-hour allotted to him to perform, he would meet his admirers backstage or outside the theatres, cheerfully shaking hands and signing autographs until the next show. Bradley was approachable and the people loved him. He was like a next door neighbor whose welcome never wore out.

Small wonder that his radio fans crowded streets, theatres and auditoriums whenever he came to town.[49]

Bradley explained his feeling about his radio audience in a later songbook:

> When I sing for you on the air, I always visualize you, a family group, sitting around the table or the radio, listening and commenting on my program. Some of you have written in and said that I seem to be talking right to you, and I am. If I did not feel your presence, though you be a thousand miles away, the radio would be cold and unresponsive to me, and I in turn would sound the same way to you.[50]

He wrote also that he had considerable doubt at first that the radio public would accept the old folk songs of the Appalachians. "It has been a great revelation to me to know that radio fans all over the United States and Canada are eager for just this type of song." He went on to say that he had tried to give a true picture of the people of the mountains by singing their songs. "To me there is a character and dignity to be found in the old mountain ballads; they represent a certain type, and are just as distinctive as the Negro spirituals."[51]

Obviously the old ballads and songs had a broader appeal than just giving a flavor of the mountains. They were either known by people throughout the country, or else they spoke of events and feelings that touched the common folk everywhere. Many persons commented that they had heard their parents or grandparents sing Bradley's songs when they were children. After the great changes during the twenties and during the upheaval of the thirties, people were comforted by the timeless ballads. Bradley Kincaid, a part of the new age of radio, was nevertheless reliably attached to the past and a strong tradition, which his listeners shared. They never tired of some of the songs. He sang "Barbara Allen" every Saturday night during the four years he was at WLS, and it was expected on his personal appearance tours.

Some fans, however, weren't just moved by the old songs. They were enraptured by the performer. While the personal appearance shows were decorous compared to the reactions of fans to later stars such as Elvis Presley, nevertheless, there were some who grew decidedly amorous on seeing for the first time the person from whom that marvelous tenor voice sprang. When Bradley's first appearance in Peoria was announced over the air, a woman who had been sending expressive and affectionate letters to him at WLS, wrote in to say that "now at last we can be together." The star panicked and was on the verge of canceling out altogether. Finally, however, he asked Dave Thompson of WLS to go along to protect his honor. He managed, according to Thompson, to escape his admirer without being compromised.[52]

After the success of the songbooks and the personal appearances, Bradley began to see that there was money in the business that he had entered reluctantly and, he thought, temporarily. He developed a system, which he followed throughout his career and which others adopted. He sang on the radio to build up a listening audience. He sold songbooks over the air, and he went on tours to sing for and sell books to his radio fans. It was a financially successful arrangement for the bleak days of the Great Depression.

After the success of the first songbook, Bradley "got into the business" of collecting and publishing the old songs. "I started to make a profession of it," he said.[53]

> The first vacation I had from singing on the radio, I came back to Berea, and Dean Edwards and I made a trip way down in the mountains of North Carolina. That's where I first met "Skyland Scotty" Wiseman [who later became a star at WLS through Bradley's influence]. I got several songs from him—like "Cindy," "Pretty Little Pink" and a bunch of those. We'd find out from the old settlers who the people were who knew the old traditional songs. We would go—I'd find somebody who'd say, "Now, Old Granny So-and-So up here in the hol-

> low, she sings a lot of these songs." Working with Miss Jameson and Professor Smith [at Berea], I'd learned to recognize the old English ballad. I'd say, "Reckon I could go see her?" "Well, I don't know. She's pretty timid." So, I'd take my guitar and go call on the old woman or man. I'd say, "They tell me you sing the old songs?" She'd say, "Oh, I don't know"—beat around the bush that way. And I'd say, "Did you ever hear so-and-so?" And I'd get out my guitar and start singing "Sourwood Mountain" or something. They'd perk up and say, "Oh, yeah, I've heard that." I'd sing for them, and that would loosen them up. Then she'd say, "Did you ever hear so-and-so?" And pretty soon she'd be singing it. I couldn't write down music, but I had a system of hieroglyphics, as it were, that I got down this and jotted down that, and when I got away, before it got cold, I would work it out on paper—get the tune straightened out, and before long I'd have another song. That's the way I collected these old ballads.[54]

Scott Wiseman well remembers Bradley's visit to North Carolina. Bradley, as a Berea student, had roomed with Scott's older brother, Earl (now a surgeon). It was natural, therefore, that he visit the Wiseman home in his quest for songs. "I sang twenty or more," Wiseman wrote, "which his assistant, Carol Edwards, took down in notation." Carol Edwards was the daughter of Dean Edwards and was then a music teacher in Detroit. "While Bradley was there," Wiseman went on, "he sang at the local high school. I sat in the audience enraptured with his smooth delivery, his clear voice and the ease with which he handled himself on stage.[55]

Bradley's collecting trips took him to North Carolina, Georgia and Kentucky. He commented that he got the "really old-timers further south, in North Carolina."[56] In his third book, he emphasized his collecting trips and ran a picture of himself sitting with his cousin Sam Hurt on the porch of his country store while Sam fiddled for him and they both pretended to smoke cob pipes made by Hurt. He got several songs from Hurt, who kept a "ballet" book. Another picture showed Bradley in Manchester, Kentucky, sitting by a man with the unusual nickname of "Shortbuckle" Roark and his four children while they sang songs learned from Mr. Roark's grandfather. On the way back to Berea, he learned "The House Carpenter" from Leslie VanWinkle at Clover Bottom, Kentucky.

Bradley had a sense of time passing and the old songs dying with the singers. And so, during the summers he would go to seek out the old songs from those who would soon pass off the scene. He wrote,

> Off the beaten trail, away from the traveled pike, in places hidden and obscure, may be the finest fountains of folk songs . . . . For the mountaineer will welcome the Singer of Mountain Songs, and playing their instruments in time and tune together, they will trade song for song and tune for tune until the day darkens into night . . . . They dig back deep in memory for the old songs that grandfather or grandmother taught them.[57]

Fans also began to send him songs that could be added to his repertory, and he swapped songs with fellow performers, such as Doc Hopkins, from whom he got "The Fatal Derby Day." His letters and collection of sheet music as well as handwritten songs show that many of the songs sent in were from composers of topical songs who wanted him to boost their song on the air. Most of these composed songs held little interest for Bradley Kincaid. The major portion of his mail was from people who knew and valued the traditional songs that were his stock in trade. He commented in his fifth songbook that "During the past five years I have received many encouraging letters from authors, professors and teachers interested in folklore, congratulating me upon the work I have been doing in this field." He is proud of his work as a collector, presenter and preserver of Appalachian ballads and songs. There is no question but that his interest in the material went beyond immediate business considerations, although he prospered at a time when many were struggling to survive.

Bradley began his recording career on December 19, 1927, with Gennett Records, owned by the Starr Piano Company. He did six sessions in Chicago for Gennett in 1927 and '28 and then three in Richmond, Indiana, in 1929. Bradley remembers that in Richmond, Gennett was using an old warehouse for a studio. "They just put me right in the middle of the floor, where there was one of those crystal mikes," he said.[58] He cut a total of sixty-three numbers for Gennett, of which thirty-eight were released on several different labels, a few under the pseudonyms of Dan Hughey, John Carpenter and Harley Stratton. Bradley reports that he knew nothing about this use of pseudonyms until he became aware of the records later.

While in Chicago, Bradley also recorded thirty-one sides for Brunswick-Balke-Collendar, which released twenty-four of them on more than a dozen labels, including labels in Japan, Canada, the British Isles and Australia.[59]

By the time Bradley left WLS in 1930, he had sixty-two songs on nineteen labels. The format at the time was the 78 rpm record, usually with one number to a side. Artists ordinarily spoke of how many "sides" they had recorded, rather than how many records. This was because the same songs in different combinations might be released on several labels.

For two of the years Bradley sang at WLS, he was a full-time student at the YMCA College. He was editor-in-chief of the college newspaper, *The Association Collegian*. The issue of December 15, 1926, carries an inspirational editorial by Bradley, entitled "The Spirit of Christmas." He also worked part-time at the La Porte, Indiana, YMCA, which was some sixty miles from Chicago. Those years must have been hectic, especially after he started personal appearances. When he graduated (with a degree in sociology), he was offered a job with the Pennsylvania YMCA organization, but he decided to stay on at WLS. He was given more responsibility at the station then, both as an announcer and a performer. His name appeared on the WLS letterhead as assistant for farm programs. As an entertainer, he toured mainly over Illinois, Indiana, Wisconsin and Michigan, except for the summers when he threw in an occasional show in the Appalachians as he traveled around collecting songs.

The Kincaid family began to grow in 1929. In fact, it doubled. Bradley and Irma had planned to name their expected baby Barbara Allen, should it be a girl, in honor of the song that more than any other had made him a star. When identical twin girls were born, they split the name, calling one Barbara and the other Allyne since Allen would hardly be a proper girl's name. News of Barbara and Allyne was expected by the fans, and so Bradley obliged, over the air and in subsequent songbooks. One fan sent the girls a dog, which they called Trixie.

WLS continued to grow in popularity and influence during the years Bradley was there. Edgar Bill was the station manager, George Biggar was program director for a portion of the time, Don Malin was music director, and Ford Rush, Harold Safford and Steve Cisler were popular announcers. John Lair came about the time Bradley left, eventually to become music director. The performers included Ford and Glenn (Ford Rush and Glenn Rowell), Grace Wilson, Ralph Waldo Emerson, Zeke Clements, Arkie, the Arkansas Wood Chopper (Luther Ossenbrink), Rube Tronson, Tommy Dandurand, Walter Peterson, Chubby Parker, Doc Hopkins, Cecil and Esther Ward, Gene Autry and George Gobel. John Lair, observing the success of Bradley's old songs, brought in more Kentucky talent: Karl and Harty (Karl Davis and Hartford Taylor), Slim Miller, Lily May Ledford, Red Foley and Linda Parker, and formed a group called the Cumberland Ridge Runners.[60] Other favorites at WLS were Lulu Belle and Scotty (Wiseman). Bradley had been much impressed with young Scott when he collected songs from him on one of his summer excursions. After he left WLS, he recommended Scott to George Biggar, who hired him. At WLS Scotty met Myrtle Cooper (Lulu Belle), another North Carolinian, and they were married.

Bradley had received offers from WLW in Cincinnati after he graduated from college. In 1930 he decided to move to WLW, although for a time he commuted back each Saturday for the WLS Barn Dance. Years later, he was to speak fondly of WLS and how well they had treated him. It appears that his popularity was at a peak there, judging from the numbers of songbooks and the volume of the fan letters he received. "I went to Chicago with $412 and four years later, I was graduated from college and had paid my way through college, had ten or fifteen thousand dollars in the bank and was driving the biggest car in Chicago."[61] However, many of the fans he developed at WLS followed him through radio to his new locations.

"I was getting a feel for show business," he said. "I went there [to WLW] and told them that I didn't want a salary. 'I just want to get some time on the air and sell my songbook and make personal appearances, and I'll give you a percentage of what I make.' They said all right, so they gave me a nice spot at 7:45 in the morning. I went on the air every morning for a month before I made any appearances." During that first month, he received 50,000 letters, and when he made his first personal appearance, there was standing room only. "And it was that way all over Ohio, Kentucky, Indiana and West Virginia, Pennsylvania and Tennessee where I played," he commented.

"I don't know how many times I played Marietta and across the river in Parkersburg, West Virginia. I played there and played there and played there."[62]

Practically all of the evidence indicated that Bradley's fans were not disappointed in him when they finally had a chance to see him in person. One, however, was dismayed about one aspect of the star's style of dress. He is Jim Comstock, editor of the widely distributed *West Virginia Hillbilly*, of Richwood, West Virginia. In the April 3, 1976, edition of his paper, he reminisced about his meeting with Bradley for an interview when he was a student at Marshall College in Huntington:

> Bradley Kincaid, remember him? The so-called Kentucky Mountain Boy who came into the American homes over WLW Cincinnati, playing his guitar and singing? I remember him well, better than who was President of the United States when Bradley was hot, or who was governor of the state even. We on Horse Ridge and Hinkle Mountain would have run him for either President or Governor, but that was long, long ago . . . .
>
> I interviewed him for the "Parthenon," Marshall College weekly newspaper. He was appearing at the Keith Albee Theatre, and Chet Anderson sent me to do a story on him.
>
> "You are a country boy, so you should get along with another country boy," Chet said. So I went to the theatre

> with a letter Chet wrote which got me in without paying. I sat through the show and at the end, I went to the singer's dressing room. He said he was in a hurry, and if I didn't mind, he would answer my questions as he changed from his stage clothes. And that became the point of my story, I became an investigative reporter. Bradley Kincaid, I reported for the world to read, country boy as he was, wore silk underwear. Granted, that was the style of the day, or at least was for the sissies and Beau Brummels. But certainly not for the country's most famous country boy! And that was my story, Chet said it was good and put it on the front page. That was better than a Pulitzer.

His stage clothing also must have caused some comment. He dressed sometimes as his interpretation of a Kentucky mountaineer, with checked shirt, suspenders, high-laced boots, but sometimes with jodhpurs which showed a leaning toward a Kentucky Bluegrass identity. Later on he briefly dressed in cowboy garb from head to foot. Off stage, he was a very natty dresser indeed, always conscious of style. He enjoyed both nice clothing and expensive cars. Marshall (Grandpa) Jones remembered that when they played at WBZ, Boston, Bradley would sometimes bring back a new car from one of his trips.

In 1931, he published his fourth songbook, *My Favorite Old-Time Songs and Mountain Ballads*, this one in a larger format. It included songs from the earlier three books that were popular with his radio audience, plus a dozen additional ones. It contained two articles on Bradley, one by WLW publicity director Natalie Giddings Halburton and the other by Berea College Alumni Director Charles T. Morgan. This songbook, published by WLW, went through four editions.

Apparently, in return for his free appearances on WLW, the station arranged personal appearances for Bradley. James W. McConnell, who later became vice president of Acuff-Rose Artists Corporation in Nashville, handled the bookings.[63]

While Bradley and Irma were in Cincinnati, two boys were added to their family; Billy was born on July 1, 1929 and Jimmy on May 31, 1931, after Bradley had accepted a job at KDKA in Pittsburgh. The songbooks continued to carry pictures of the Kincaid family, and Bradley regularly broadcast news of the children's development. He referred to Irma as "The Girl Friend" and gave her credit for the musical notations in his books.

For the next ten years he moved from one station to another, staying approximately a year and a half at most places, singing for a while on good time slots until the people in the station's area became familiar with him and then publishing another songbook and beginning personal appearances. George Biggar commented on this practice:

> The showmanship methods developed at WLS were used whenever possible in the presentation of Bradley Kincaid's air programs on the other stations where he was featured.
>
> Insisting upon "across-the-board" fifteen minute program scheduling was most important in building up Bradley's audience acceptance on all of the stations where he was featured. He no doubt did much to establish this scheduling practice as it concerned other "traveling minstrels."
>
> The above method of building up acts with mass audience appeal was quite prevalent for several earlier years of radio. Stations were very much pleased to have good performers fill their time at little expense to them.[64]

"He never went to one station and wore himself out," John Lair mentioned. "He never let it [the area] become saturated."[65] This practice of moving from one station to another discomfitted some of his true-blue fans. Some wrote to the effect, "Well, Bradley, at last we've found you. We've been searching for you on stations all over the country. How about staying put for awhile?"

From WLW he went to KDKA in Pittsburgh (which had established an early barn dance show) and thence to WGY in Schenectady. His next stop was WEAF in New York City and the NBC Red Network. From there he went to WBZ in Boston. He was to spend nearly ten years in the East, though he doubted at first that he would be popular so far from the Southern Mountains. He did personal appearance tours throughout the

New England states and was very popular with audiences there.[66]

Until the mid-thirties, he had mostly traveled alone on personal appearance tours. But just before he was in New England he teamed up with Louis Marshall Jones, an entertainer from Kentucky, and Joe Troyan, who did a bashful country boy act with harmonica. Marshall Jones sounded old, according to Bradley, even at twenty-four years old, so he began calling him Grandpa. He went on to become a popular performer on the Grand Ole Opry and the TV show, "Hee Haw," still wearing the high-top boots that Bradley had bought in Kentucky and given him in New England.

Grandpa Jones remembers fondly those years with Bradley and Joe Troyan.

> We started in the early part of 1935, I believe. I first met him when he came to Akron to play a show there. I had another boy with me by the name of Harmonica Joe [Troyan], and he saw our act and liked it and asked how we would like to meet him in West Virginia and then go with him to New England. We had to talk it over, but we met him in Clarksburg for about three days there and went on to New England. We played WBZ in Boston. We were supposed to play three months on the air before we played any dates, so that we could build up our popularity. Well, we played two weeks, and we had so many inquiries we played Gardner, Massachusetts—three or four shows in a little theatre in one day—and we never did get all of the people in. About every date from then on was that way. There were just a few places we didn't do well. In most places there were capacity crowds.

> I had the good fortune of playing all up and down the New England coast with Bradley. I'd watch the audience when he'd sing a ballad, and you could hear a pin drop. They wanted to know how the story went, and his voice was perfect for the song. I've watched them many a time, and they were sort of spellbound when he'd sing those songs.

> Here's how I got the name "Grandpa." We were playing all over New England. We'd drive back at night because we had to

> do a morning show, in the early morning, I'd be tired, and he'd [Bradley] say, "Get up to the microphone. You're like an old grandpa." The people got to thinking I was old. I sounded like I was eighty.
>
> Bradley had a fine sense of humor, which he has right now. He would tell a few jokes on stage in between his songs. We had a big time in Boston. We had an apartment—the three of us—and we did some cooking. Bradley would make the coffee. His family was still in New York, on Long Island at the time.[67]

Joe Troyan holds a great respect for Bradley from those New England years. He remembers him as a "first class guy, a real gentleman, honest, sincere and thoughtful."

> He was a teacher. I learned much from Bradley about show business and about many other things. He set an example for me to follow .... He watched over Grandpa and me like a hen over her peeps. I think Grandpa and I set an example for Bradley too. When we joined Bradley, neither of us smoked. Bradley smoked one pack a year. He said, "If you boys don't have to smoke, neither do I." And he quit. That's the kind of guy Brad was.
>
> Brad, Grandpa and I were doing a personal appearance on a Sunday in North Adams, Massachusetts. Because of the distance (175 miles) to Boston, and since we were scheduled to be on the air over WBZ at 7:00 a.m. Monday, Bradley asked the theatre manager if it would be all right with him if we could do our stage show early so as to get an early start for our long trip back to Boston. The manager agreed. Bradley turned to Grandpa and me and said, "Boys, we can't lose any time. As soon as we finish on stage, you both hurry and get the mike, the instruments, clothes, etc. and put them in the car. I'll see the manager, check out and be with you in a jiffy. We can't lose any time.
>
> We didn't lose any time. Brad was out to the car and behind the wheel in ten minutes, and we took off. After driving for about an hour, Bradley said, "Boys, I think we're lost. I think I saw a state sign reading 'Vermont.' " We kept going for a

> few miles and stopped at a gas station. Bradley went in for directions and came out in two minutes and said, "Boys, we're near Bennington, Vermont. We went the wrong way on Route 2." Grandpa looked at Bradley and said, "I knowed it all the time." Bradley said, "Well, Grandpa, why didn't you say something?" Grandpa said, "You didn't ask me." After all that we drove 100 miles and not a word was spoken.[68]

WBZ and WBZA in Springfield, Massachusetts, were owned by the Westinghouse Corporation, and they both carried the broadcasts of Bradley and his friends. They occasionally broadcast their programs from WGY in Schenectady, another Westinghouse station, when they were nearer to that city than to Boston on personal appearance tours. The programs were then piped to WBZ and WBZA.

Bradley, Grandpa and Joe played together for nearly three years. Then Joe received an offer from another entertainer. Troyan remembers Bradley's kindness and understanding. After saying that he knew that both Grandpa and Joe would do well in the country music field he said, "I would never stop anyone from trying to better himself."

> And then I had to fight back a tear or two when Brad put his hands on my shoulders, looked me in the eyes and said, "Bashful Joe, don't ever change your act. It's original, and I want to wish you and your partner the best of everything, and I hope you make it big. But Joe, if something happens, and things don't work out, remember, you always have a job with me. No matter where you are, call me or wire me and I'll mail transportation money . . . . " That was my good friend Bradley. I'll never forget that meeting.[69]

Grandpa Jones also went his way, but he was to join Bradley's tent shows later when they both were at WLW and the Grand Ole Opry.

After singing briefly at WTIC in Hartford, Connecticut, Bradley returned to WGY in Schenectady, moved to WHAM in Rochester, and then returned to WLW. During these years he did not vary his method of operation—doing a radio show, selling songbooks and making personal appearances—until in 1941, while he was at WHAM, he started the Circle B Ranch at Avon,

New York, and he also started a tent show. The ranch was really a fairgrounds rented by Bradley, with a performing stage, cowboys and occasionally bucking horses. The tent show idea consisted of various acts. For example, Foster Brooks, the comedian who now does a drunk act, worked for Bradley out of Rochester. Bradley continued the tent shows at other stations—WLW and WKRC in Cincinnati and WSM in Nashville.[70]

Back at WLW in 1942, Bradley toured county fairs and theatres with the Boone County Jamboree. His fellow entertainers were Grandpa Jones, Curly Fox and Texas Ruby, Merle Travis, The Prairie Sweethearts, The Delmore Brothers, Roy Starkey, Hank Penny and Dolly Good. These shows were organized and presided over by "Happy Hall" O'Halloran. Bradley remained at WLW for three years. In 1944, he sang at WKRC in Cincinnati, before moving on to WSM and the Grand Ole Opry.

While he stayed longer at WSM than at any other one station he was not as popular there in comparison to the other Opry stars as he was at the other stations where he was the most popular performer. Mainly, this was because of the great changes that were taking place in country music at the time, which Nashville led. He had this to say about the Opry:

> To tell you the truth, while I was there for five years, I never did feel at home on the Grand Ole Opry like I did at WLS. When I went down there, there was Roy Acuff who had been established for years, and Ernest Tubb and a few others like that. They were so well established that nobody else could get in. At least that was the attitude I developed. I'd say that I was just fairly popular on the Grand Ole Opry—not like I was on WLS. It may have been a change in taste, for I was very old-fashioned.[71]

"I think Bradley was wrong about not being accepted," said Jimmy Driftwood (Morris), who followed him at the Opry as a singer of folk songs. "I think he must have had something happen that made him feel that way."[72]

When asked about how well Bradley was accepted at the Opry, Grandpa Jones said:

> Well, at that time, Hank Williams was big and a lot of others. Hank was getting hit after hit, and he didn't have time

> for anybody. But people like Sam and Kirk McGee respected Bradley very much. Bradley's songs, you've got to really listen to them because they're slow and tell a story. That's the reason Jimmy Driftwood had problems at the Opry too. They really have to listen. He [Driftwood] said they got to hand-slapping when he got out there, and he really couldn't do it. Bradley felt he didn't get as good a hand as others who were so popular. I thought he did well. It was just a different audience at WSM than the audience in New England was.[73]

Ramona Jones, Grandpa's wife, who often plays with her husband, does not agree with Bradley on his popularity at the Opry:

> I didn't feel that way about it. We loved Bradley. He might have been one of many, and there were so many other musicians here then who had been here longer—were better established. I got the feeling that he wasn't very happy here. He really had a following, though. You have no idea how popular Bradley Kincaid and his houn' dog guitar was—and is even today .... He still has a great name .... Maybe by the time he came to Nashville, he wasn't going so strong, and some of the newer kinds of music were taking over. I'm sorry to say that more of the band sound was taking over by the time I knew Bradley.[74]

Both Roy Acuff and Eddy Arnold remember Bradley as a careful businessman. "Bradley didn't play out a lot," Acuff remembered. "He always seemed to be more of an executive. Most of the boys were trying to make it on the road, but [with] very few thoughts about the business end the way Bradley did." Arnold remembered him as "an intelligent, educated man, who knew how to look at a profit-and-loss sheet and make his investments accordingly." Arnold went on to talk of Bradley's popularity and the fact that he had listened to him when he was a kid on the farm.[75]

While Bradley might not have been the most popular star at WSM with those who admired the new country sound, he was still the favorite of his old fans, who had followed him from station to station, and of many new fans. He traveled throughout the South, mainly with his own and others' tent shows, with such persons as Grandpa and Ramona Jones and Uncle Dave Macon. Bradley talked about trips with Uncle Dave:

> We went out into Oklahoma. We played Claremont where Will Rogers is from, and Uncle Dave was on the show. I can remember hearing him say [quoting Rogers], "I'll tell you we've got some great men in Congress. We've got about the best men money can buy up there." He was crazy about country ham. He'd go into a restaurant, pull that ham out of his pocket. A waitress would come around, and he'd say, "Fry me some of that with some eggs."[76]

Ramona Jones talked about the tent show:

> I worked on his tent show for a few months. Grandpa and I were not married then. We got married a little bit later after we both left the tent shows. I don't know how successful they were. It may have been a time when tent shows were going out. There may have been a time when they were more successful than they were that particular year. That was about 1944, shortly after he came to WSM.[77]

Mrs. Jones recalls playing through eastern Kentucky and particularly remembers riding through Bradley's native Garrard County and having him show her the church he helped to build as a brick carrier when he was a boy.

In 1950, Bradley decided to hang up his guitar. His feelings about the changing sound in Nashville no doubt influenced his decision. As bands with their electric instruments became more popular, interest in traditional styles waned. His friend Ramona Jones thought this change in musical taste, or in the kind of music that was promoted then, was a factor in his decision to quit as a singer. She expressed what were probably his feelings:

> I'm really sorry that they brought in the drums and the background music at the Opry . . . . I'm sorry that it hasn't kept more of its charm and uniqueness it had during the early years—more down to earth. I'm sorry that they have the drums so loud, steel guitars so loud, background music so modern . . . . The Opry is trying to please all types of listeners, and I think they've lost a lot of their uniqueness.

> I'm sure that's why he went into retirement as soon as he did. He probably was a bit disgusted at the way music was going at the time.[78]

The immediate reason for his leaving Nashville, however, was that he had joined partners to build a radio station in Springfield, Ohio–WSSO. Here is how he told the story:

> The station was losing money hand over fist, and every month, I'd get a letter from the manager of the station saying, "Your allotment for the deficit this month will be $1500 or $1000 or $500! Every month! So I said, "I'm going up to Springfield and either put that thing to sleep or do something.[79]

In Springfield he was able to "get hold of a real rip-snorter of a time salesman," and they put the station in the black in two months. He managed the station for five years and then he and his partners sold it to a group from Dayton. They moved the station to that city and opened it under the new call letters of WAZI.

He announced that he was retiring from show business, played golf for a year, was bored by retirement and decided to accept an offer to return to WLW. "I noticed my old guitar case was looking pretty bad," he explained. "I went down to a Springfield music store to get a new case and met one of the best salesmen I've ever seen. He sold me a new case and then talked me into buying the store."[80] The music store was named Morelli's, but eventually its name was changed to Kincaid's. He operated it for a time, but gradually turned it over to his son, James ("Jimmy"). Bradley continues to spend a couple of hours a day at the store, but most of the time he says, "I'm out playing golf or down at the YMCA jogging."

At this writing, Bradley Kincaid is a healthy, tanned, silver-haired gentleman of eighty-four, who sometimes drives a convertible and cracks a fast joke. He serves on the Traditional Music Committee of Berea College and helps plan and appears on an annual Celebration of Traditional Music. In 1974, he sang to a standing ovation at Mac Wiseman's Old-Time Music Festival at Renfro Valley, Kentucky. All of his fans marvel that his voice is as sweet and clear and friendly as it was when they first heard him. Ramona Jones commented, "I am amazed at his health and how many songs he remembers."

He and Irma now have ten grandchildren. They still live in Springfield, but Bradley talks nostalgically of moving back to Kentucky.

IV

Bradley continued to publish songbooks and to cut records throughout his career. They stand as evidence of his large performing repertory of over 300 songs. He, or publishers, included a few songs in his songbooks, however, which he did not actually perform.

His first (six printings) through third songbooks were published in Chicago, while he was with WLS. The fourth was published at WLW, Cincinnati, the fifth at KDKA, Pittsburgh, the sixth in New York but with no station indicated and the seventh at WBZ, Boston. The Southern Music Publishing Company of New York published Number 8 in 1937. In the same year, a second edition, expanded from twenty to fifty songs was issued, and in 1938, Southern Music reissued this fifty-song collection as a "Deluxe Edition," with the Number 8 designation dropped from the cover. Though Bradley privately published his Number 9 from Garden City, New York, in 1939, he counted the "deluxe" edition of Number 8 as his tenth songbook.[81] Number 11 was published at WHAM, Rochester in 1940. Folio Number 12 was published in 1941 by Peer International Corporation, which was organized by Ralph Peer who also managed the Southern Music Publishing Company. The last songbook, Number 13, was published by Bradley in Nashville while he was with WSM. In a note to his "radio friends" in this book, he mentioned that he had been in radio more than twenty years, indicating a publishing date in 1947 or 1948.[82] (See Appendix B for titles and publication dates and places of all songbooks.)

The books were in various sizes, ranging from 7" x 6¾" to 9" x 12". The covers pictured Bradley, usually in casual clothes —work shoes, checked shirt, suspenders—with some artwork depicting mountain scenes in the background. On the cover of his twelfth book, however, he is dressed up from head to foot in cowboy togs with a smaller picture of him on a pinto horse. This change in image was a reflection, no doubt, of his "Circle B Ranch" show at Avon, New York, while he was at WHAM, Rochester. Inside pictures frequently presented a bespectacled and dressed-up Bradley, with other shots of his home and family. Earlier books pictured his birthplace, mountain scenes, Berea College and Bradley collecting songs. Later books emphasized his family, carried pictures and messages from station managers and sometimes pictures of announcers and fellow performers. Book II carried fifteen "homey" poems by his friend "Bud" Rainey of WTIC, Hartford.

In the books that Bradley published privately or through various radio stations, he did not claim ownership of his versions of folk songs. However, Southern Music and Peer International added Bradley's name as author or owner of many folk songs. This action shows the hand of Ralph Peer, who developed a practice of copyrighting traditional songs for his companies or the artists who sang them. Bradley commented to this writer that he never felt right about receiving royalties from songs he felt should be in the public domain. But apparently neither Bradley nor others such as A.P. Carter ever protested very loudly to Peer about this practice.

Irma Kincaid transcribed the melody lines of the songs for the printers on the earlier songbooks. In some of the later books, she or others added piano accompaniment and guitar chords. Archie Green suggests that musicians at Peer International and Southern Music may have done the transcriptions for the books they published.[83]

Some of the books were well-prepared and printed. Others may have been rushed into print, since they contain typographical errors and other mistakes in the lyrics. Some of the music does not adequately describe the versions that Bradley sang, although it was probably meant only to suggest the basic melodies and not Bradley's style. In the transcriptions of the songs included in this book, John Forbes has considered printed transcriptions, but he has compared them with recordings of Bradley's rendition of each and has attempted also to capture some of the nuances in Bradley's singing style.

Bradley cut his first record on December 19, 1927, for the Starr Piano Company.[84] He had nine more sessions with Starr by October 4, 1929, a total of sixty-three sides, of which thirty-eight were released. These numbers were issued on Gennett, Champion, Silvertone, Supertone and Superior. Some of the songs were issued under the pseudonyms of Dan Hughey, John Carpenter and Harley Stratton. This was a common practice in the early recording industry. Usually the artist was not consulted in this practice, and Bradley was not. He says he first knew about it when someone asked, "Why are you hiding your light under a bushel?" Between November 22, 1929, and December of 1930, he cut thirty-one sides for Brunswick-Balke-Collender Company. Of these, twenty-four were released on Brunswick, Melotone, Conqueror, Vocalion, Banner, Oriole, Romeo, English Panachord, Irish Decca, Australian Regal Zonophone, Sterling (Canada), Coral (Japan) and MCA (Japan).

Bradley changed to RCA Victor for three sessions—September 14, 1933, February 14, 1934 and May 7, 1934, all in New York—cutting a total of twenty-eight sides. All twenty-eight were released on Bluebird, Montgomery Ward, Electradisk, Sunrise and Australian Regal Zonophone. He then did three New York sessions with Decca, cutting six sides in September of 1934, one side on November 28, 1934 (probably to replace a number from the earlier session that was not suitable to be issued, but which instead was paired with a later transcription), and seven sides on November 30, 1934. These numbers were released on Decca and Irish Decca.

After moving to Nashville, Bradley recorded two sides for the Bullet Recording and Transcription Company, probably in 1944, released on the Bullet label, and eight sides for the Majestic Record Company, probably in 1945. After leaving WSM, he recorded four sides for Capitol Records in Springfield, Ohio, in 1950.

All of the numbers recorded up to 1950 were for 78 rpm records. However, several of these numbers were later released on 33 1/3 rpm long-playing disks. From the RCA Victor takes, Camden and Victor released four LPs that included Bradley's songs. The Majestic recordings were released on a Varsity LP,

Bradley Kincaid Singing American Ballads and Folk Songs and on a Design LP entitled *Cowboy*.

In February of 1963, after Bradley had been retired from singing for thirteen years, Ed Manney, of Bluebonnet Records in Fort Worth, Texas, contacted him about doing some new recordings. After considering the matter for a month and talking it over with his family, Bradley consented. His reason for recording, he said, was that his grandchildren and most younger people had never heard his recordings. Also he felt that some of his songs might die with him unless he could get them circulating again on new records. He flew to Texas on August 6, 1963, and spent five days, Tuesday through Saturday, recording 162 songs, which were more than half of all the songs he is known to have sung. Twenty-three of these were songs that he apparently had not used professionally before. Some may have been learned after his retirement. From these recordings, Bluebonnet released seventy-four on six LP albums, all titled *Bradley Kincaid, "The Kentucky Mountain Boy," Mountain Ballads and Old-Time Songs.*[85]

In 1973, Bradley recorded twenty-six numbers in Springfield, Ohio, for McMonigle Music, Inc. (6201 Santa Monica Blvd., Hollywood, California 90038) which were issued on both the McMonigle Round Robin Label as LPs: *Bradley Kincaid: The Mountain Boy* (BK 101A/BK 102B) and *Bradley Kincaid: Family Gospel Album* (BK-3/BK-4). Neither album has a release date, but the first was issued around 1974 and the second around 1978. McMonigle also issued a 45 rpm record on the Round Robin label (LM-104A/LM-104B) of "The Legend of the Robin's Red Breast" and "There's a Red Light Ahead" from the same Springfield recordings.

Old Homestead Records (Box 100, Brighton, Michigan 48116) released an LP in 1976 from some of Bradley's early recordings. It is *Mountain Ballads and Old-Time Songs* (OHCS-107). Bradley considers this to be the best of recent releases because the numbers selected were recorded when his voice was at its best and his guitar playing good.[86] (See Appendix C for complete discography.)

Bradley feels that he never got a fair return from the many

records he made. He remembers that he usually got the minimum musician's wage after the Musicians Union was established, but he believes he was cheated on royalties. He tells of cutting twelve sides for Victor for which he was never paid at all. He did not receive royalties from the Camden, Victor and Varsity LPs on which his earlier recordings were reissued. Bluebonnet paid him for his expenses to Fort Worth with a check that bounced. While he later received a good check for these expenses, he reports, "I never received a dime for royalties."[87] As a result of the sometimes slipshod or outright tricky methods of operation that he observed in some of the record companies, Bradley does not have a good feeling about the record-making part of his career. However, his is an impressive discography, and these records contain most of his fine repertory.

Bradley's repertory consisted of 332 songs, judging from those that appeared in his songbooks, on his many recordings and in two large loose-leaf notebooks that he kept to refresh his memory. In addition to songs, he also recited poems, sometimes with guitar accompaniment in the manner of talking-songs (and he kept another notebook of these poems, together with jokes and other humorous material). He pointed out several songs in his books published by Peer Southern and Peer International that he never actually sang, and these have not been included in the check-list of his songs. Into his eighth decade he can quickly identify songs mentioned at random, such as how he had learned them, and then can proceed to sing them. He mentioned also that he knew some songs that he could not use on the air or stage. His repertory is impressive, perhaps as large as any ever documented. As a comparison, Bascom Lamar Lunsford, North Carolina singer, collector and festival promoter, recorded from memory around 320 songs, tales, singing games and the like in two sessions, one at Columbia University and the other at the Library of Congress. Lunsford's is perhaps the largest memory collection ever recorded. Bradley probably could not have sung all of his large repertory from memory at one time, but he has a prodigious memory and had a hunger for new songs to enrich and vary his collection.

As stated earlier, he got a good many songs from his father

and mother, from such relatives as his cousin Sam Hurt of near Paint Lick, Kentucky, his Aunt Stanley Maxwell of Clay City and his Uncle Ben Kincaid,* from fellow entertainers, fans and songbooks. He wrote several and used other composed songs that had an old-time flavor (See Appendix A for a listing of songs with Bradley's comments and other identifying notes).

Many of his favorites were English and Scottish ballads that can be found in the Child collection.[88] Examples are "Barbara Allen," "Fair Ellen (Lord Thomas and Fair Ellender)," "The Gypsy Laddie," and "The House Carpenter." There were also other types of ballads from the British Isles, such as "Froggie Went A-Courtin'," "A Pretty Fair Maid," "Darby's Ram," "Father Grumble," and "Young Rogers the Miller." He sang many American ballads also, for example, "Pearl Bryan," "Darling Cory," "The Lily of the West," and "The True and Trembling Brakeman." He had a rich collection of lyric folk songs, many from the British Isles: "The Cuckoo is a Pretty Bird," "Fair and Tender Ladies," "The Foggy Dew," "I Gave my Love a Cherry"–and many native ones as well–"Cindy," "I Love Little Willie," "Free Little Bird," and the like. He had many humorous songs, such as "Sourwood Mountain," "Ain't We Crazy," "The Cat Came Back," "Methodist Pie," "Rattler," and "What'll I Do With the Baby-O," and he had a large collection of sentimental songs, of fairly recent composition. Some of these songs, which were very popular in early radio days, were "Put My Little Shoes Away," "Twenty Years Ago," "There Never was a Pal Like Mother," "My Little Home in Tennessee," and "Give My Love to Nell." He sang hymns, but there are only a few that appear in his songbooks and on recordings.

Some of the songs that he did not use often were black spirituals and so-called race songs, although he sang spirituals when

*Ben Kincaid, who died at eighty-one in 1971, played over WFIV in Hopkinsville, Kentucky, in the early 1930's with a group called "Hiram Scrunch and his Happy Family." He called himself "The Briar Hopper." Bradley thought he was the B.F. Kincaid who recorded for Gennett, although D.K. Wilgus, a folk scholar, does not agree.

he was with the YMCA quartet in Chicago. "I used to sing them," he said. "My father used to sing a lot of them."

> But when I got into radio, I couldn't use them. They were a reflection on the Negro. In fact, I sang "Kitty Wells" one time. The first line is, "You ask me why this darky weep" and this woman called me up and gave me down the road for it. After that I sang, "You ask me what made the fellow weep." I've got a big repertory of Negro songs that were written back in the 1800's—minstrel-like songs. I couldn't use them.[89]

While he had the conventional attitudes of white people of the time, this recollection indicates that he was sensitive to offending black people. Most other white entertainers of the time frequently used songs that did not portray blacks favorably.

Bradley wrote several songs. The most successful was "The Legend of the Robin's Red Breast." A fan, Blanche Preston Jones, sent him the words, and he wrote the tune and afterwards used it regularly. During World War II he wrote two patriotic songs, "Captain Bill" and "I Won't be Back in a Year, Little Darling." He also wrote or co-wrote such songs as "Fifty Years from Now," "Some Little Bug is Going to Find You," "Fond of Chewing Gum," "The Innocent Prisoner," "Little Darling Don't Say we are Through," "Now the Table's Turned on You," "Red Light Ahead," "Cornpone and Molasses," "Sleepy Head," "That Old Tintype Picture," "Little Red Rooster and the Old Black Hen" and "Mammy's Precious Baby."

Top, WLS National Barn Dance Halloween party, October 1929. Bottom, publicity photos as WLS star and with Irma and the twins, Barbara and Allyne.

V

Bradley made many fans during his career, and he influenced a lot of musicians, scholars and producers of musical shows, probably many more than ever acknowledged his influence. Several well-know persons have spoken of his effect on them. D.K. Wilgus, folk scholar at the University of California at Los Angeles wrote:

> When I say that Bradley was the first person to stimulate my interest in American folksong, I am not really being personal. This kind of stimulation is the essence of Bradley Kincaid's contribution to the recognition of the value of folksong by those in mainstream American culture as well as to its continuing performance by traditional singers.
>
> . . . my first real memory of him is being pulled out of a theatre about 1931 in Portsmouth, Ohio, by my uncle, who finally found me as I was watching the third of Bradley's shows that day.[90]

Wilgus goes on to comment that Grant Rogers, a folk singer from the Catskills, was influenced by Bradley, as were the Jacobs Family of Antigo, Wisconsin, who sing "Barbara Allen" as they learned it from him on the radio.[91]

Scott Wiseman wrote fondly about Bradley:

> Bradley had a great influence on me and is largely responsible for my decision to make a career in music instead of teaching . . . . He and my brother were roommates at Berea. After Bradley had been on radio for a few years, he came to our home in North Carolina looking for songs to add to his collection . . . .He told me that I was a good enough singer to be on radio and offered to take me back to Chicago and help me get started. While Bradley was there, he sang at the local high school. I sat in the audience enraptured with his smooth

> delivery, his clear voice and the ease with which he handled himself on stage. I became a fan at once and started copying Bradley's style . . . . He talked with the program director at WLS Chicago and I eventually got on the barn dance a few years later.[92]

George Biggar wrote Bradley in 1975 that "Scotty will forever be grateful to you for the good words about him that you wrote [to] me way back when. He admired you very, very much and you were his inspiration to get into the 'Big Time.' "

Another Wiseman–Mac–of Nashville fame, also paid tribute to Bradley,

> Bradley Kincaid had a big influence on me. I didn't realize it at the time, though. I just liked what Bradley did. It was beyond my wildest dream to be part of the business so I didn't try to copy anybody or copy a style. I'm afraid in later years I found I was more greatly influenced by what Bradley did in my creative years than I ever realized.[93]

Another admirer was Doc Hopkins, a versatile singer from Renfro Valley, Kentucky, who followed Bradley at WLS and sang there and at other stations for many years,

> Bradley Kincaid was my choice above all singers I heard in those days. I played the same style that he did and many of the same songs. I've been accused of sounding like Bradley . . . . We were similar because we featured the same kind of genuine American folksongs and played a guitar accompaniment. Bradley was on the air a few years before I was, on the same radio station. I became acquainted with him and he introduced me to radio work.[94]

Ralph Rinzler wrote that the Monroe Brothers acquired their early performing repertory from listening to Bradley Kincaid and other early artists on records and over WLS.[95]

"I certainly learned a lot of songs from him," Grandpa Jones reported. "He could sit down and sing a lot of songs that I hadn't even heard, and I'd been with him for several years.[96]

Charles Wolfe, in a recent article, wrote of Bradley's influence on Grandpa Jones.

> The years Marshall spent with Bradley Kincaid did a lot for

him both personally and professionally. He credits Bradley with giving him a sense of dignity for his calling: a feeling that singing was a respected and respectable vocation. Professionally, Bradley was a major influence on Marshall's developing repertoire; in addition to genuine traditional ballads and songs, Bradley enjoyed great success with old sentimental ballads like "I'm Tying Up the Leaves So They Won't Fall Down." His delivery style was simple, straightforward, unadorned, and somewhat restrained; his listeners could hear the message of his song clear and true. In those days, before Grandpa had started playing the banjo and developing his exhuberant style, a singing style like Bradley's was vastly appealing. Today Grandpa asserts he "doesn't have the voice" for sentimental ballads and love songs, but he has always been fond of the genre, and some of his fondness undoubtely comes from these years with Bradley. In fact, Grandpa's first big hit song as a single was his composition "Answer to Maple on the Hill," which he popularized . . . in 1937, the year he left Bradley Kincaid.[97]

Ramona Jones emphasized his influence on her and Grandpa as well as on other commercial singers:

Yes, he had a great influence. I know he did on Grandpa, and he did on me also, because I loved the old folk songs and began to realize the importance of the old songs, once I had known Bradley and heard him talk about them. I think he probably knows more authentic folk songs than anyone I know - he and John Lair at Renfro Valley. I'd put them more or less in the same category, so far as knowing authentic folk songs.

I always looked up to him because I knew he was very intelligent . . . . I wish I had been able to have gone to college and to have been able to express myself like Bradley did, for I thought he could express himself so well, and still can to this day. I always admired him . . . . I became very fond of Bradley, and I admired him a lot and loved the old songs he did. And I still love them today. Grandpa sings his songs all of the time. He has always been a gentleman to me.[98]

The fans wrote in by the thousand to sing Bradley's praises:

After you left WLS we have not been able to follow your

> programs, until recently I picked your cheery voice from WLW . . . . I did get you faintly from Atlanta, Georgia, and I wish to let you know how much I enjoyed it . . . . Please do not make excuses for singing the sad songs. They are beautiful. . . .
>
> Radio programs are slipping, in my opinion. We do not get the really good music that we did a few years ago. There is so much jazz and silly jokes that it is a real treat to sit back and enjoy those beautiful sad sweet numbers.
>
> Radio means so much to us rural people as we cannot afford expensive concerts or shows, thus radio brings entertainment to fill our long winter nights. (Dora M. Pernow, Basco, Wis., Dec. 8, 1934)

And the fan letters are still coming, such as these:

> How well I remember the later twenties or early thirties when I was a high school teenager, and my father bought our first dollar down and a dollar a week radio. All the neighbors would gather in on a Saturday night to listen to the barn dance and your mountain ballads were the highlight of the evening. Also, I would hear you every morning before leaving for school. My mother ordered some of the little books that you published, and I wish so much that I still had them. That must have been at least forty-five years ago.
>
> It would be wonderful to hear you singing those sweet songs again—so different from the so-called "Country Sounds" of today.
>
> Remembering you so fondly and hoping that somehow this letter will reach you, I remain,
>
> Still a Bradley Kincaid Fan.
>
> (Mrs. J.B. Cothran, Greeneville, S.C., 1975)
>
> I have admired you since your early days on radio at WLS. Then later at WSM Nashville. It must be [because of] a combination of your life in the hills of Kentucky and the type of songs you sing, and I guess most of all the way only you can sing them . . . . I am your best fan. (Floyd Murphree, Besse-

mer, Ala., May 18, 1975)

> I hope you will be able to understand the reasons why I am writing to you, and forgive my boldness, but in 1930-32 I listened to you every afternoon—no matter what—at 3:30 p.m. when you would come on the air singing your theme, "In the Hills of Old Kentucky." I was a kid ten to twelve years old in love with those good old songs and country music . . . . I've never forgotten the happiness your music brought. (Mrs. H.B. Duncan, Beaumont, Tex., Apr. 8, 1975)

> I have wanted to write to you and let you know that I surely did enjoy your most wonderful voice and songs. You were always my favorite of all the artists, so I shall always have fond memories of the Kentucky Mountain Boy and his Houn' Dog Guitar . . . . It seems that you just never did a bad song. I loved them all. I used to play a guitar, and I listened to your records and played them just as you did. I really felt proud when I played right with you on the records. When friends and I discuss the GOOD OLD DAYS on radio, your name always comes up and I tell that you were always my favorite, and always will be . . . . (Hope Hinds, Dixon, Ill., Nov. 13, 1975)

> It is now forty years ago since I saw you on the stage of a theatre in New Bedford, Massachusetts. I remember you coming out the side door after the show and I talked to you in person and I thought it was a great thrill to meet you there. I have never forgotten you. (Clarence J. Anderson, Falmouth, Mass., Sept. 27, 1975)

Mr. Anderson, a carpenter, who drove several hundred miles out of his way on a trip with Mrs. Anderson from Falmouth, Massachusetts, to Florida in 1977, just to talk with this writer certainly demonstrates the devotion many fans have, but he also helps to give reasons for Bradley's popularity:

> It was one of the big thrills of my life to meet Bradley in person. From that day on I listened to Bradley more than anyone else I could hear on the radio. If I knew of a program he'd be on, I'd quit everything else and listen to him. The rest of the time—I could just as well throw the radio out the window.

> I completely lost track of him about 1945 and didn't know whether or not he was living or what had become of him, until someone put a little ad in *Good Old Days Magazine*—something pertaining to Bradley. I wrote explaining my interest and asking if he was still living and how I might get in touch with him. I got a letter back immediately telling about a write-up in the Springfield *Sun*, and I found out about Bradley's store, and I wrote him there.*
>
> Bradley came along just when we were getting radios in our homes. I was always interested in just the mountain ballads of Kentucky and that type of music, and I've never had any interest whatsoever in any other kind of music. I'm a New Englander. I was born and brought up on Cape Cod. Believe me, I should be right here in Kentucky! I remember my mother—she came from a Scandinavian background—I would tune in this kind of music on my early battery radio, and she was quite put out with me. She'd say, "Why do you listen to that kind of stuff all of the time?" It was the only kind of "stuff" I would listen to. Nobody stood out in my young days like Bradley. His music made me think so much of the early pioneers coming to this country. Their songs were telling the story of their struggle. They are not commercial songs like the junk that is on the air today. The songs represent what the people did. There is a lot of feeling in those songs. Modern music has no feeling—at least not for me.
>
> I've just never found another singer like Bradley.[99]

There is no question that Bradley Kincaid was the most popular singer at WLS and certainly one of the most popular at a number of other stations in different parts of the country where he played during the nearly twenty years after leaving WLS. The fan letters, the numbers at personal appearances, the sale of his songbooks and the numbers of records sold attest to this fact. Several persons have tried to answer the obvious questions

*One other fan, thinking Bradley was not still living, wrote to the music store asking for information on "the late Bradley Kincaid." Bradley received it and replied with, "What was I late to?"

about his popularity: Why did folks like him? Why were they so moved by the old songs he sang, even those who had not been brought up on ballads and sentimental songs? What was there in the happenings of the late 1920s and the 1930s that may have been a factor in attraction to the old songs? How did his music relate to the developing country music? What was his influence? Here are some comments from knowledgeable people in response to some of these questions.

Dr. Cratis Williams, former Acting Chancellor, Graduate Dean and Professor of English at Appalachian State University, Boone, North Carolina, and a ballad scholar:

> There had been a little interruption in the routine of mountain life during World War I. Many mountain folk had gone out and come back, and many of them had touched the twentieth century as it was being lived then. And along came the Victrola that gave them a chance to renew their interest in their own traditions—plus the new radio stations. And everything was just ripe for it. The Depression came, and I think the emphasis shifted from urban to rural life on a national basis, and that in itself encouraged a revival of interest in the traditional.
>
> People were buying country music of all sorts—Gid Tanner and the Skillet Lickers and Charlie Poole. Those were great favorites. Doc Boggs appeared, and along came Bradley Kincaid with them, and people were already interested in finding on the radio or on records the songs they themselves had been singing all of their lives, or that they had heard or liked. Bradley had a fine repertory, to begin with, and had apparently done his research well. He always presented excellent variants of these songs. He brought a fine voice and skill with his instrument. He sang with vitality and verve, and there was a time, as I look back, that he was the foremost ballad singer, or country singer, in the country.
>
> He could sing a folk song or ballad very well, and one who was in the tradition could recognize that it was well done. Now in contrast to that, I knew some other people attempting to sing traditional ballads, who presented them as if they were grand opera, and when they did that the folk did not respond

because they were not in the tradition.

> My recollection is that he was a man with a shock of curly dark hair and bright eyes—a handsome fellow—and I'm sure that this in itself added to his stage presence when he went around to present his programs. He had very fine enunciation. It was superb, which I thought probably was owing to more education than the average folk singer had.[100]

Scott Wiseman, now living in Spruce Pine, N.C. when he and his wife Lulu Belle are not in Raleigh where she is a member of the North Carolina legislature:

> In my opinion there were a number of reasons for Bradley's tremendous success, among them not the least is that he was in the right place, at the right time, and he was ready to make good use of opportunities. Radio was the new craze that was sweeping the country. Until Bradley brought his guitar to the studio and sang . . . there had scarcely been any "country music" on the air. It was a happy discovery that this was the entertainment people of all ages and walks of life loved to hear in their homes. So Bradley was a pioneer, and he made the most of it. His fine voice, his poise, clean-cut good looks and friendly, outgoing personality helped a great deal. The Christian background and self discipline learned at Berea were big assets. His willingness to spend long hours collecting and memorizing songs and his ability to concentrate were marks of a true professional . . . . Bradley made an immense contribution to folk and country music.[101]

Grandpa Jones was in a position to observe Bradley's success in New England and other such places far removed from the Southern Mountains:

> Bradley learned these songs in the hills the way they should have been sung. A lot of people hadn't heard them that way. By that I mean that he sang them authentic, more than a lot of people, and maybe that was the reason. His voice was good—he still has a good voice—and I think that helped. It was just pleasant listening . . . .
>
> I think at that time they hadn't heard that kind of music,

or not for a long time. A lot of songs as Bradley sang them were from the old countries, and there were a lot of people in New England who knew about them.[102]

Don Malin, former music director of WLS and now with Belwin-Mills Publishing Corporation in Melville, New York:

I do like to recall that it was through programs broadcast from WLS, Chicago, that Bradley brought to many Americans their first knowledge of the beautiful American and Anglo-American fold music which is the heritage of the South . . . .

Bradley was always modest about his talents and achievements and best of all he preserved his respect for the integrity of these songs. When you heard him sing "Barbara Allen," "The House Carpenter," "Sourwood Mountain" and many others you had the feeling that you were hearing authentic folk-music, not commercial "Country-Music."

So far as I know, Bradley has always maintained this sense of integrity so that the material he reclaimed supplements the collecting and editorial activities of such American Folksong authorities as George Pullen Jackson, Charles F. Bryan and others.

You will be correct in ascribing to Bradley Kincaid a considerable share of the credit for awakening the interest of Americans to their own folk music. He started a trend which, helped by others, had and still has considerable influence on the musical activities of America, particularly in our schools.

The interest in folk music expanded and ultimately led to what has now become an important American industry—Country Music. Bradley may thus be considered as one of the pioneers in this field, although I suspect that he does not approve of all the features of the Country Music scene.[103]

Karl Davis, of the "Karl and Harty" team at WLS, who worked for WLS Radio until his recent death:

Hartford Connecticut Taylor and I (Karl and Harty) had been picking the guitar and mandolin a lot and singing a little

> as we grew up in Mt. Vernon, Kentucky. In the spring of 1930 when the star of the famous National Barn Dance came to our hometown and asked us to come to WLS it was something you would only expect in a dream. Thus we had the great honor and pleasure of working with Bradley Kincaid.
>
> Bradley Kincaid was so instrumental in heading folk and country music down the right paths toward the greatness it has reached. He was one of the first to sing folk songs on radio and when he sang them they sounded so good . . . . He was big in the city and he was big in the country.
>
> Bradley's voice was loaded with simple, plaintive appeal. I remember his being dignified and polished and his songs came out just that way. He resented the word "hillbilly" and when he did he was only sticking up for our kind of music and all of us who were in it. He wanted our music and us to have a lot of respect and to be on a high level.[104]

Reuben Powell, founder and operator of the Renfro Valley Tape Club for many years and a serious student of folk and country music, a native Kentuckian, now living in Springfield, Ohio:

> I have always believed that his popularity was due to a combination of voice, type of material, and the "right time" in history. He particularly had and still has a very good voice, particularly suitable for the type of song he sang. So his voice must be considered his greatest asset even though he never used it emotionally the way some performers do. Although I was, and am, one of Bradley's admirers of the first order, I always (even in 1928) felt like he was a popular song singer adapted to my type songs. His voice training I suppose was the reason for his style.
>
> I think it is fairly certain that Bradley's popularity was not due to his personality, at least up close. He has always been aloof from his fans; however, that may not have affected his popularity for most of the thousands of fans couldn't have gotten very close to him anyway. His guitar playing certainly didn't influence many fans. He was considered a mediocre

picker in the hey-day of his popularity.

It is true that Bradley was the first to bring purely mountain music to radio. The songs were familiar to many in the audience even though they may have forgotten the words. The material reminded them of earlier time, somewhat a nostalgic reaction similar to that going on today. As to that period in history, the mountains of Kentucky, Tennessee, North Georgia, North Carolina, East and West Virginia have furnished much of the labor supply for the factories in the North for the past 100 years . . . . I can testify that nothing makes a hillbilly more homesick than a familiar song of his youth when he is far from home. That reaction is double on an outdoorsman confined to a factory assembly line for economic reasons. I must say that I have no answer for his popularity on the plains and in New York State, where his popularity was very great.

As to his contribution to folk and country music. I think his gathering and publication, in addition to recording and performing the mountain ballads was a very great contribution to widening the distribution and understanding of mountain folk music. I think his contribution, although he was not the first to gather such material, and not the most scholarly, was as great, if not greater than any other living man. Although he did not sell as many records as the Carter Family, he was much better known in the early days due to his work on radio which reached a very wide audience. For that reason, and because he advertised his material as mountain ballads where the Carters tried to disguise their use of the material by changing words, phrases and tunes and taking credit for composing the material, I think his influence was greater than the Carter Family. I am sure many will take issue with me, but you asked for my opinion.

You cannot find a [folk-country] performer that started in the decade following Bradley that did not use some of his material in the beginning. Many of them will admit that Bradley influenced them . . . . I suppose that Jimmie Rodgers was the most imitated man ever in the country field. . . but Bradley must have been just about as imitated because . . . Bradley worked some of the biggest stations in the U.S. and was as

> well-known as any performer of his time.[105]

William Tallmadge, Professor of Music at the University of Buffalo and later at Berea College and an authority on folk music:

> Bradley's approach to his material and his singing style remind me of the approach the Fisk Jubilee singers took. Vernon Dalhart's singing voice and Bradley's voice seemed similar. Both probably appealed to the same type of audiences. Today we tend to like a more traditional vocal production, but in 1926 Dalhart and Kincaid were probably on the right track for great popularity, and for spreading their material abroad (of course Dalhart had no material to spread really).[106]

Stephen A. Cisler, who was the announcer for Bradley's show at WLS, now in the electronics business in Louisville, Kentucky:

> Simple melodies are usually the most beautiful. A new thing appears in its simplicity and catches public fancy if it is basically of quality. So it was with Bradley Kincaid and his bringing out of the early radios the simple beauty of mountain music.
>
> This was new to radio in those days. It stood out from the ricky tick dance bands, the concert tenors and sopranos, and the talkers who made up the programs. So here was Bradley with a trained and pleasing voice. His songs were melodious. They told a story. His diction projected every word well. This was in sharp contrast to other programs. His small talk on the air added to his human attraction to the listener. He made no claims to having written the old songs. He was not surrounded by bands of fiddlers or yodelers. He brought peaceful music to a growing new medium at the right time. Hence his popularity in early Chicago days. This expanded with his broadcasts from other major centers. No one man has done more to popularize or introduce sincere and genuine country music than has Bradley with his mountain songs . . . . Yes, people like simple and good things . . . so they liked Bradley and his music . . . everywhere.[107]

Bradley Kincaid quit show business when interest in folk

music, his main love, was at a low ebb. Most of us in the years following World War II were in a progressive mood. We yearned for new things, and the young people especially were into new music, new ideas, new ways. Folk festivals, for example, the Mountain Dance and Folk Festival in Asheville, North Carolina, had their smallest audiences in the late forties and early fifties. The folk revival, in the vehicle of hootenannies, had not yet come. After the folk boom of the sixties and seventies did come, Bradley was urged by many people to take down his guitar again and share his songs with a new audience, but he declined. In fact he innocently sold his guitar for much less than its worth to a person who came into the music store one day looking for just that type of Martin 000-45. Only in recent years has he become involved in festivals as a senior advisor and occasionally a somewhat reluctant singer. He has been generous with his time to interviewers and recorders. But he is still somewhat modest and shy about his accomplishments.

He overcame great handicaps to get an education. He accidentally stumbled into the world of radio music. He became an instant success just by singing the songs he had learned in his native Kentucky from ordinary people. While he had studied voice and worked constantly to improve his repertory, his success was due mainly to his modest and pleasing personality and his feel for and knowledge of a rare treasure of folk music. It was a natural Bradley Kincaid with mountain songs who caught the attention and enduring loyalty of a host of fans. He took the gifts he had received from a culture that is generally thought of as deficient in many ways and, because he was where he was at a certain time in history, he became a professional musician, and many persons and the music industry have benefitted richly from his career.

NOTES

1. Interview with Bradley Kincaid by Dorothy Gable, November 12, 1967. Courtesy of the Country Music Foundation, Nashville, Tenn.

2. Interview with Bradley Kincaid by Ruth Wilson, undated. Courtesy of the Country Music Foundation.

3. "Old Ballads Hit on Radio," Jackson, Miss., *News* (September 13, 1929).

4. Gable interview.

5. Interview with Bradley Kincaid by Loyal Jones in Berea, Ky., April 24, 1974.

6. Kincaid interview, April 24, 1974.

7. Interview with James Ralston by Loyal Jones in Berea, Ky., April 28, 1977.

8. Ed Ford, "Bradley Kincaid . . . . The Man Who's Called Country Music's Pioneer," *Berea Alumnus* (January-February, 1975), p. 7. Also author interview.

9. Kincaid interview, April 24, 1974.

10. Ralston interview, April 28, 1977.

11. Letter from J. H. Ralston, May 22, 1975.

12. Gable interview.

13. Gable interview.

14. Bradley Kincaid, *My Favorite Mountain Ballads and Old-Time Songs* [Book No. 5] (Pittsburgh: KDKA, 1932), p. 9.

15. Gable interview.

16. Gable interview.

17. George C. Biggar, "The National Barn Dance," *Country & Western Scrapbook*, edited by Thurston Moore, 14th edition (no date or location given on material).

18. Letter from Don Malin, June 5, 1975.

19. Gable interview.

20. Bill C. Malone, *Country Music, U. S. A.* (Austin: University of Texas Press, 1968), pp. 37-39.

21. Robert Shelton and Burt Goldblatt, *The Country Music Story* (Secaucus, New Jersey: Castle Books, 1966), p. 27.

22. Malone, pp. 40-41.

23. Malone, p. 43.

24. Malone, pp. 43-45.

25. Archie Green, "Bradley Kincaid's Folios," *JEMF Quarterly*, 12 (Summer 1977), p. 25.

26. From Loyal Jones' research on Bascom Lamar Lunsford and interviews with Buell Kazee and Mrs. Dennis Taylor.

27. Malone, pp. 107-10.

28. George C. Biggar, "Facts on Radio Broadcasting (1920-1964)," (DeKalb, Illinois: WLBK-AM & FM, May, 1964). Mimeographed paper.

29. Biggar, "Facts."

30. Malone, p. 36.

31. James F. Evans, *Prairie Farmer and WLS: The Burridge D. Butler Years* (Urbana: The University of Illinois Press, 1969), pp. 160-61.

32. Evans, p. 165.

33. Malone, p. 72.

34. Evans, pp. 214-16.

35. Malone, pp. 72-73.

36. Evans, p. 223.

37. Malone, pp. 35-36.

38. Malone, p. 46.

39. Gable interview.

40. Gable interview.

41. Wilson interview.

42. Letter from George C. Biggar, April 12, 1975.

43. Letter from Clementine Legg Segal, June, 1975.

44. Gable interview.

45. Ford, p. 6.

46. Telephone interview with Marshall Jones by Loyal Jones on September 21, 1976, and interview in Berea, Ky. on October 28, 1978.

47. Marshall Jones interview, October 28, 1978.

48. Gable interview.

49. Segal letter.

50. Kincaid, (Book No. 5) p. 3.

51. Bradley Kincaid, *Mountain Ballads: Old Time Songs* [Book No. 8] (New York: Southern Music Publishing Company, 1937) Foreword.

52. Evans, pp. 216-17.

53. Gable interview.

54. Kincaid interview, April 24, 1974.

55. Letter from Scott Wiseman, April 18, 1975.

56. Kincaid interview, April 24, 1974.

57. Bradley Kincaid, *Favorite Old Time Songs and Mountain Ballads* [Book No. 3] (Chicago: WLS, 1930), p. 8.

58. Wilson interview.

59. See Appendix B.

60. Malone, p. 71.

61. Kincaid interview, April 24, 1974.

62. Kincaid interview, April 24, 1974.

63. Shelton and Goldblatt, p. 221.

64. Biggar letter.

65. Interview with John Lair by Loyal Jones at Renfro Valley, Ky., April 30, 1974.

66. Gable interview.

67. Marshall Jones interviews.

68. Letter from Joe Troyan, October 7, 1976.

69. Troyan letter.

70. Letter from Bradley Kincaid, March 31, 1976.

71. Kincaid interview, April 24, 1974.

72. Interview with Jimmy "Driftwood" Morris by Loyal Jones in Timbo, Ark., June 12, 1976.

73. Marshall Jones interviews.

74. Telephone interview with Ramona Jones by Loyal Jones on September 21, 1976, and interview in Berea, Ky., October 28, 1978.

75. Joe Derek, "Bradley Kincaid is Legend in Grand Old Opryland," Springfield *Sun* (March 24, 1975).

76. Interview with Bradley Kincaid by Reuben Powell in Springfield, O., January 21, 1971.

77. Ramona Jones interviews.

78. Ramona Jones interviews.

79. Kincaid interview, April 24, 1974.

80. Ford, p. 6.

81. Green.

82. Green.

83. Green.

84. See Appendix C.

85. Schedule and explanation of Bradley's Bluebonnet recordings was prepared by Katherine Smith, who worked for Bluebonnet, and supplied by Eddie Nesbitt.

86. Telephone conversation with Bradley Kincaid by Loyal Jones, January 20, 1978.

87. Kincaid telephone interview, January 20, 1978.

88. Francis James Child, *The English and Scottish Popular Ballads* 5 vols. (Boston: Houghton Mifflin, 1884-1898; rpt. New York: Dover, 1965).

89. Kincaid interview, April 24, 1974.

90. D. K. Wilgus, "Bradley Kincaid," *Stars of Country Music: Uncle Dave Macon to Johnny Rodriguez*, Bill C. Malone and Judith McCulloh, eds. (Urbana: University of Illinois Press, 1975), p. 86.

91. Wilgus, pp. 93-94.

92. Wiseman letter.

93. Tom Henderson, "Mac Wiseman." *Pickin'* (August, 1975), p. 5.

94. Interview with Doc Hopkins by Sidney Farr in Berea, Ky., October 25, 1975.

95. Ralph Rinzler, "Bill Monroe," Malone and McCulloh, pp. 109-10.

96. Marshall Jones interviews.

97. Charles Wolfe, "Grandpa and Ramona Jones: Two Lives, One Music," *The Devil's Box*, (December 1, 1979), pp. 3-20.

98. Ramona Jones interviews.

99. Interview with Mr. & Mrs. Clarence J. Anderson by Loyal Jones in Berea, Ky., July 1, 1977.

100. Interview with Cratis D. Williams by Loyal Jones in Berea, Ky., March 19, 1976.

101. Wiseman letter.

102. Marshall Jones interviews.

103. Malin letter.

104. Letter from Karl Davis, April 24, 1975.

105. Letter from Reuben Powell, April 24, 1975.

106. Interview with William H. Tallmadge by Loyal Jones in Berea, Ky., 1977.

107. Letter from Stephen A. Cisler, May 17, 1975.

Top, Bradley with Joe Troyan and Marshall "Grandpa" Jones in Boston, publicity shot while he was in New England. Middle, with George Biggar, WLW program director, about 1940. Bottom, with the WKRC road show from Cincinnati, 1943.

Clockwise from top: in cowboy attire for Circle B Ranch program in Rochester, marquee for Boone County Jamboree, at a war bond rally in Cincinnati's Fountain Square and photo taken while at the WSM Grand Ole Opry.

Henry Schofield Studio

Les Leverett

Top, Bradley and Eddie Arnold (left of photo) participating in a wartime radio show, with the Fisk University Jubilee Singers and the Nashville Symphony. Bottom, presenting his "Houn' Dog" guitar to Dorothy Gable, director of the Country Music Museum and posing with his old friends Grandpa and Ramona Jones and their daughter Alisa at Nashville's 1978 Fan Fair.

Phil Ledford

Bob Parriott

Bradley in recent years, in the Kincaid Music Store in Springfield, Ohio, and at the Berea College Celebration of Traditional Music.

PART II

A SELECTION OF BRADLEY KINCAID'S SONGS

TRANSCRIBER'S NOTE

The following songs represent the variety in Bradley Kincaid's repertory of songs: ballads, both authentic folk ballads from the British Isles and America and known compositions that have entered the oral tradition; lyric folk songs and humorous numbers from Britian and America; sentimental songs of relatively recent origin; and two of Bradley's compositions. The transcriptions represent, as closely as possible, Bradley's tune and text. The task was one of correct text underlay consistent with current musical convention. An asterisk at the beginning of the chord symbols represent those suggested in Bradley's songbooks when they were present. Most of the selected songs had no such indications, and the chord symbols are only suggestions based upon internal melodic evidence. In a few instances the given text did not fit with the musical note values given in the songbooks. Bradley Kincaid's own recordings of these songs were consulted and his versions or variants were used to assure accurate results. Please note that major chords are given in upper case letters, minor ones in lower case.

John M. Forbes

FAIR ELLEN

2. He went and called his merry May men, by
one, by two and three.
Go saddle and bridle my coal black steed, fair
Ellen I must see.

3. He dressed himself in cloth so fine, put on a
mantle in green,
And every village that he rode thru he was
taken to be some King.

4. He rode till he got to fair Ellen's hall, he
jingled at the ring,
And none so ready as fair Ellen herself, she
rose and let him in.

5. Good news, good news, fair Ellen he said, good
news I've brought to you,
I've come to ask you to my wedding, for married
I must be.

6. Bad news, bad news, Lord Thomas she said,
bad news you've brought to me,
You've come to ask me to your wedding, for
married you must be.

7. She went and called her merry May men, by
one, by two and three.
Go saddle and bridle my milk white steed,
Lord Thomas' wedding I'll see.

8. She dressed herself in cloth so fine, put on a
   diamond ring,
   And every village that she rode thru she was
   taken to be some queen.

9. She rode till she got to Lord Thomas' hall, she
   jingled at the ring,
   And none so ready as Lord Thomas himself,
   he rose and let her in.

10. Lord Thomas, Lord Thomas, is this your
    bride? She's very dark and dim,
    When you could have married as fair a fine
    lady as ever the sun shined on.

11. The Brown girl had a little pen knife, it was
    both keen and sharp,
    Betwixt the long rib and the short, she pierced
    Fair Ellen's heart.

12. Lord Thomas, Lord Thomas, are you blind, or
    can't you very well see,
    And can't you see my own heart's blood come
    trinkling down my knee?

13. He took the Brown girl by the hand and led
    her thru the hall,
    And with a sword cut off her head and kicked
    it against the wall.

14. He threw the sword upon the floor; it flew into
    his breast.
    Here lies three lovers all along in a row, Lord
    send their souls to rest.

15. Go dig my grave under yonder green tree, go
    dig it both wide and deep,
    And bury fair Ellen in my arms and the
    Brown girl at my feet.

THE TURKISH LADY

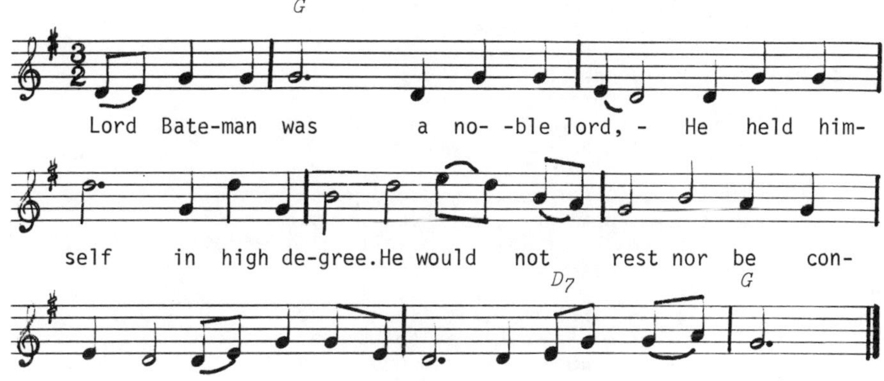

2. He sailed east and he sailed westward,
   Until he reached the Turkish shore.
   And there he was taken and put in prison;
   He lived in hopes of freedom no more.

3. The Turkish had one only daughter,
   The fairest creature eye ever did see.
   She stole the keys to her father's prison,
   Saying, "Lord Bateman I will set free."

4. "Have you got houses? Have you got lands, sir?
   Or do you live at a high degree?
   What will you give to the fair young lady,
   That out of prison will set you free?"

5. "I've got houses and I've got lands, love,
   Half of Northumberland belongs to me,
   And I'll give it all to the Turkish lady
   That out of prison will set me free."

6. "Seven long years I'll make a vow, sir,
   Seven more by thirty-three.
   And if you'll marry no other lady,
   No other man shall be married to me."

7. She took him to her father's harbor,
   And gave to him a ship of fame.
   "Farewell, farewell, to thee, Lord Bateman,
   I fear I ne'er shall see you again."

8. For seven long years she kept her vow, sir,
   And seven more by thirty-three.
   She gathered all her gay fine clothing,
   Saying, "Lord Bateman I'll go and see.

9. She sailed east and she sailed westward,
Until she reached the English shore.
And when she came to Lord Bateman's castle,
She lighted down before the door.

10. "Are these Lord Bateman's gay fine houses,
And is his Lordship here within?"
"Oh, yes, oh, yes," cried the proud young porter,
"He has just taken his young bride in."

11. "What news, what news, my proud young porter,
What news, what news, have you brought to me?"
"Oh, there is the fairest of all young ladies
That ever my two eyes did see."

12. "She's got rings on every finger,
And on one of them she has got three,
And she's as much gold around her middle,
As would buy Northumberland from thee."

13. "She tells you to send her a slice of cake,
And draw her a glass of the strongest wine,
And not to forget the fair young lady,
That did release you when close confined."

14. Lord Bateman rose from where he was sitting,
His face did look as white as snow,
Saying, "If she is the Turkish lady,
With her, love, I am bound to go."

15. Oh, then, he spoke to the young bride's mother,
"She's none the better nor worse for me;
She came to me on a horse and saddle,
And she shall go back in a carriage and three."

16. "Your daughter came here on a horse and saddle,
And she shall go back in a chariot free.
And I'll go marry the Turkish lady,
That crossed the roaring sea for me."

THE HOUSE CARPENTER

2. If you've had an offer of a king's daughter fair,
   I think you're much to blame;
   For I've lately married a house carpenter,
   And I think he's a nice young man.

3. If you'll forsake your house carpenter
   And come along with me;
   I'll take you where the grass grows green,
   On the banks of the deep blue sea.

4. If I'd forsake my house carpenter
   And go along with you;
   And you'd have nothing to support me on,
   Oh, then what would I do?

5. She dressed herself in rich array,
   All from her golden store;
   And as she walked the streets all around,
   She shone like a glittering star.

6. She called her baby unto her
   And gave it kisses three,
   Saying, "Stay at home, my pretty little babe,
   And be your father's company."

7. We had not sailed more than two weeks,
I'm sure it was not three;
'Till this fair maid began for to weep,
And she wept most bitterly.

8. Are you weeping for your house carpenter,
Or for your golden store?
Are you weeping for that sweet little babe,
That you never shall see any more?

9. I'm not weeping for my house carpenter,
Nor for my golden store;
I'm weeping for my sweet little babe,
That I never shall see any more.

2. There was a young man came courting there,
Bow down.
There was a young man came courting there,
Bow and balance to me.
There was a young man came courting there
And made the choice of the youngest fair,
I'll be true to my love
If my love be true to me.

3. He bought the youngest a fine fur hat,
Bow down.
He bought the youngest a fine fur hat,
Bow and balance to me.
He bought the youngest a fine fur hat,
The oldest sister didn't like that,
I'll be true, etc.

4. O Sister, O Sister, let's go to seashore
And see the ships come sailing o'er.

5. As these two sisters walked 'long the sea brim
The oldest pushed the youngest in.

6. O Sister, O Sister, pray lend me your hand
And you can have my house and land.

7. O Sister, O Sister, pray lend me your glove
And you can have my house and land.

8. I'll neither lend you my hand nor my glove
For all I want's your own true love.

9. The miller got his fishing hook
And fished the fair maiden out of the brook.

10. O Miller, O Miller, here's five gold rings
To push the fair maiden in again.

11. The miller's to be hung on his old mill gate
For the drowning of poor Sister Kate.

A PRETTY FAIR MAID

2. "I have a sweetheart on the ocean,
For seven long years, has been to sea;
And if he be gone for seven years longer,
No other man shall marry me."

3. "Perhaps your sweetheart he is drownded,
Or perhaps he's on some battlefield slain,
Or perhaps he's married to some fair, fine lady,
Perhaps he'll ne'er return again."

4. "O, if my sweetheart he is drownded,
Or if he's on some battlefield slain,
Or if he's married to some fair, fine lady,
I'll love the one that's married to him."

5. "But my sweetheart he is neither drownded,
Nor is he on some battlefield slain,
Nor is he married to some fair, fine lady,
For he is by my side again."

6. He put his hands into his pockets,
His fingers they were long and slim;
And unto her he drew a locket,
And at her feet his knees did bend.

7. She put her hands upon his shoulder,
And he her favor did implore;
"I've come to claim you for my darling,
And I shall roam the seas no more."

8. As down the path they walked together,
His arm around her waist so trim,
He told to her a loving story.
The maiden gave her heart to him.

THE GYPSIE LADDIE

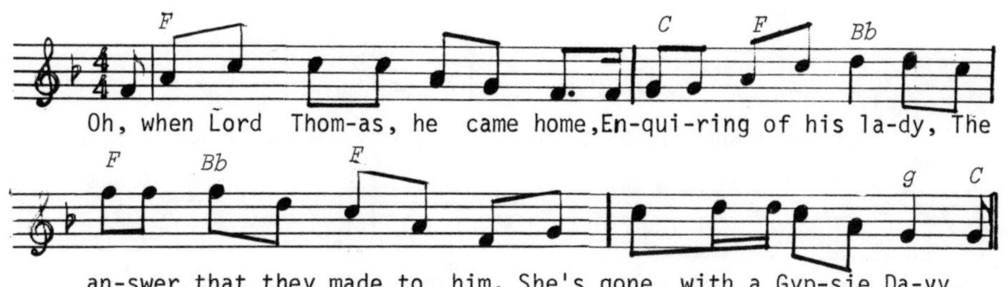

2. It's he caught up his old grey horse,
And he caught up his pony.
He rode all night and he rode all day,
Till he overtook his doney.

3. It's come go back my dearest dear,
It's come go back my honey,
It's come go back my dearest dear,
And you'll never lack for money.

4. I won't go back my dearest dear,
Nor I won't go back my honey.
I wouldn't give a kiss from my Gypsy's lips
For you and all your money.

5. It's go pull off those snow-white gloves,
A-made of Spanish leather,
And give to me your lily-white hand
And bid me farewell forever.

6. It's she pulled off those snow-white gloves,
A-made of Spanish leather
And gave to him her lily white hand
And bade him farewell forever.

7. I once did have so many fine things,
Fine feather-beds and money,
But now my bed is made of hay
And the Gypsies a-dancing around me.

FROGGIE WENT A-COURTIN'

2. He rode up to Miss Mousie's door,
   Hit it so hard that he made it roar.

   (Sing "um huh" after each line.)

3. Then Miss Mousie let him in
   And the way they courted was a sin.

4. He took Miss Mousie on his knee,
   Said "Miss Mousie won't you marry me."

5. "Before, kind sir, I can answer that,
   I'll have to ask my Uncle Rat."

6. Uncle Rat gave his consent,
   The Weasel wrote the publishment.

7. Uncle Rat he went to town
   To get his niece a wedding gown.

8. What does he get for the wedding gown?
   A piece of hide of an old grey-hound.

9. Where shall the wedding supper be?
   Way down yonder in a hollow tree.

10. What shall the wedding supper be?
    Dog-wood soup and catnip tea.

11. First came in was a little white Moth,
    And she spread on the table cloth.

12. Next came in was a bumble bee
    Totin' his fiddle on his knee.

13. Frog came swimming o'er the lake,
    And he was swallowed by a big black snake.

14. A little piece of corn bread lying on the shelf.
    If you want any more you can sing it yourself.

PRETTY POLLY

2. "Polly, pretty Polly, come go along with me,
   Let's take a little walk before we married be."

3. He led her thru the valleys and hollows so deep.
   At length pretty Polly began for to weep.

4. They went a little farther, she chanced to espy.
   She saw her grave dug and the spade lying by.

5. "Oh, William, Oh, William, Oh, William," said she,
   "I'm afraid you're going to take my sweet life away
   from me."

6. "Poor Polly, Poor Polly, you've guessed it just right,
   I was digging your grave the best part of last night."

7. He pierced her thru the heart and the blood it did flow,
   And into the grave her fair body did throw.

8. His ship was lying ready, all on the seaside,
   He swore by his Maker he'd sail the other side.

9. And whilst he was sailing, in full heart's content.
   The ship sprung a leak, to the bottom she went.

10. And there was pretty Polly all in a gore of blood.
    In her lily-white hands was an infant to God.

11. "Oh, William, Oh, William, you've no time to stay,
    There's a debt to the Devil that you're bound to pay."

AWAY SHE WENT GALLOPING DOWN THE LONG LANE

2. I mounted her upon my horse like a lady,
So scornfully she looked me into the face,
Saying, "I know by your meaning you're highly mistaken,"
And away she went galloping down the long lane.

3. "Oh, gentlemen lend me one of your horses,
'Till I follow after her down this long lane,
And if I overtake her I'm sure for to make her
Be glad to return me my horse back again."

4. She turned herself 'round and she saw me a coming
She instantly drew her pistol in hand.
Saying, "This is my skill and my skill I'll fulfill
And if you don't stand back you are a dead man."

5. "Oh, here are five guineas I think you deserve them,
If you will return me my horse back again,"
"You keep your five guineas, perhaps you will need them."
And away she went galloping down the long lane.

6. "Oh, where have I spent all my days out in roving,
Oh, where have I spent all my money in vain,
And where is the woman that was born to deceive me?"
Away she went galloping down the long lane.

DINAH

2. As Dinah was out in the garden one day,
Her father came to her and to her did say,
"Go dress yourself, Dinah, in gorgeous array,
I'll bring you a husband both gallant and gay."

3. "Oh Father, dear Father," the daughter replied,
"To get married just now I've not made up my mind;
One half of my fortune I'd freely give o'er,
If you'd let me live single a year or two more."

4. "Oh Daughter, dear Daughter," the father replied,
"If you won't accept to be this young man's bride,
I'll will all my fortune to the nearest of kin,
You sha'nt reap the benefit of one single thing."

5. As the merchant was walking the garden around
He found his dear Dinah lying dead on the ground;
A cup of cold poison sitting close by her side,
And wrote on the cup, "by poison she died."

6. He fell down beside her and felt of her heart,
Crying, "from my dear Dinah I never will part;"
He kissed the cold corpse ten thousand times o'er,
And called her his Dinah, but she was no more.

DARBY'S RAM

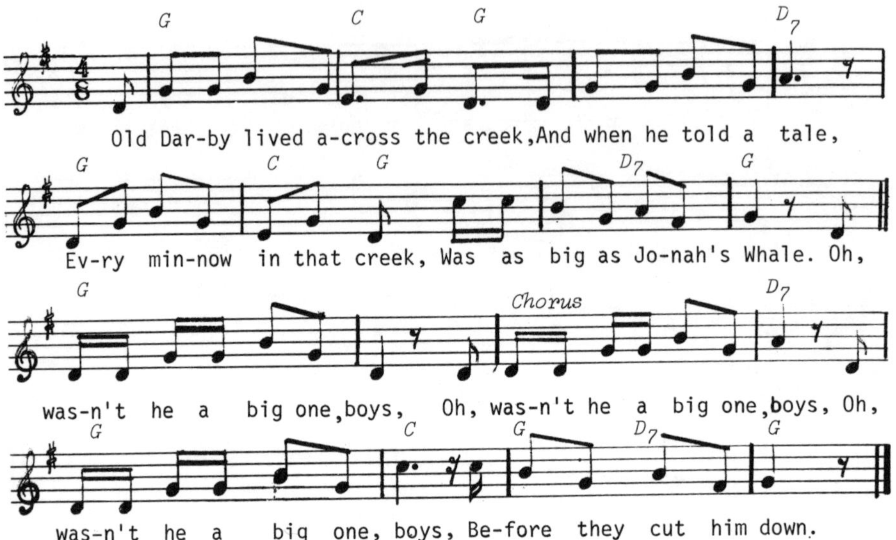

2. My daddy had an old buck sheep,
   And then you'd hear him say,
   One of the finest rams, sir,
   That was ever fed on hay.

3. He had four feet to walk, sir,
   He had four feet to stand;
   And every foot he had, sir,
   Would cover an acre of land.

4. The wool that grows on this ram's belly,
   Reaches to the ground.
   'Twas sold to Mr. Dobson,
   For fourteen hundred pounds.

5. The wool that grows on this ram's back,
   Reaches to the sky;
   The eagles built their nest in it,
   For I heard the young ones cry.

6. This old ram he had a horn,
   That reached up to the moon;
   A man went up in January,
   And never got back till June.

7. The length between this old ram's eyes,
Was forty yards complete;
And there they built the pulpit,
For the Methodists to preach.

8. The butcher man that cut him down,
Was washed away in the blood;
And the little boy that held the bowl,
Was drownded in the flood.

DARLING CORIE

2. Dig a hole in the meadow,
Dig a hole in the ground,
Dig a hole in the meadow
And lay Darling Corie down.

3. Wake up, wake up, Darling Corie,
What makes you sleep so sound?
The highway robbers are coming
And they'll tear your playhouse down.

4. Last time I saw Darling Corie
Was on the banks of deep blue sea,
Two pistols around her body
And a banjo on her knee.

5. Wake up, wake up, Darling Corie,
And go get me my gun;
I ain't no man for trouble,
But trouble has just begun.

6. Dig a hole in the meadow,
Dig a hole in the ground,
Dig a hole in the meadow
And lay Darling Corie down.

DOG AND GUN

2. The time was appointed the wedding to see.
The squire chose a farmer his waiter to be.
No sooner had the lady the waiter espied,
He inflamed her true heart, "Oh! my true heart,"
she cried.

3. Instead of getting married she went to her bed.
The thought of the farmer still ran thru her head.
The thought of the farmer still ran thru her mind,
And how to gain him she was quickly to find.

4. A coat, vest and pants did the lady put on.
Away she went hunting with dog and with gun.
She hunted all around where the farmer did dwell,
Because in her true heart she loved him so well.

5. Often she fired but nothing she killed.
At length the young farmer came into the field.
To talk with him there it became her intent,
With her dog and her gun on to meet him she went.

6. "I thought you'd have been to the wedding," she cried,
"To give to the squire his beautiful bride."
"Oh, no," said the farmer, "The truth to you I'll tell.
"I couldn't give her to him 'cause I love her so well."

7. It pleased the young lady to see him so bold.
She gave him her glove that was flowered with gold,
Saying, "Take this I found it as I did come along.
I found it while hunting with dog and with gun."

8. The lady went home with a heart full of love,
And gave out the news that she had lost her glove,
And the one that will find it and bring it to me,
The one that will find it his bride I will be.

9. It pleased the young farmer to hear of the news.
Straightway with the glove to the lady he goes,
Saying, "Here honored lady, I have just found your glove.
Will you be so kind as to grant me your love?"

10. "My love it is granted," the lady replied.
"I love the sweet breath of the farmer," she cried.
"I'll be mistress of dairy and milking of cow,
While my jolly young farmer goes whistling to plow."

11. And when they were married she told of the fun,
How she courted the farmer with dog and with gun,
"And now that I have him so close in my snare
I'll love him forever, and vow I don't care."

THE LITTLE MOHEE

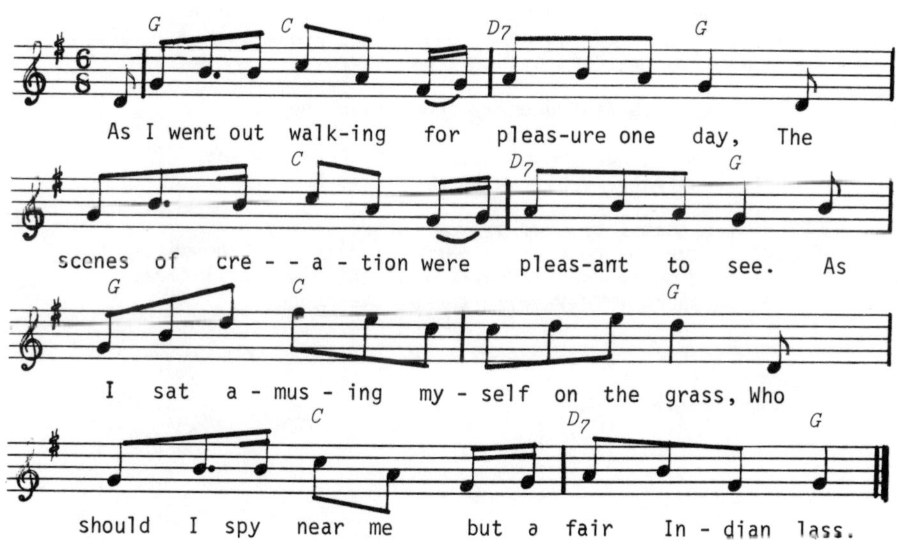

2. She sat down beside me, and took up my hand,
Saying, "You are a stranger and in a strange land.
But if you will follow, you're welcome to come,
And live in a cottage that I call my home."

3. The sun was fast sinking far o'er the blue sea,
When I wandered alone with my pretty Mohee.
Together we wandered, together we roamed,
Till we came to a cottage in the cocoanut grove.

4. Then this kind expression she made unto me,
"If you will consent, sir, to stay here with me,
And go no more roving across the deep sea,
I'll teach you the language of the Little Mohee."

5. "Oh, no, my fair maiden, that never could be,
For I have a sweetheart far over the sea;
I'll never forsake her, for I know she loves me,
And her heart is as true as the Little Mohee."

6. So one fair morning, one morning in May,
To this fair maiden these words I did say,
"I'm going to leave you, so farewell, my dear,
My ship sails are spreading, and home I must steer."

7. The last time I saw her she was down on the strand,
And as my boat passed by her, she waved me her hand,
Saying, "When you get home, dear, to the one that you love,
Remember the maiden in the cocoanut grove."

8. And as my boat landed on my own native shore,
With friends and relations around me once more,
I stood and gazed around me, but none could I see
That was fit to compare with my Little Mohee.

9. The girl that I trusted proved untrue to me,
So I'll turn my course backward far o'er the blue sea.
I'll turn my course backward, from this land I'll flee,
I'll go spend my days with the Little Mohee.

THE HUNTERS OF KENTUCKY

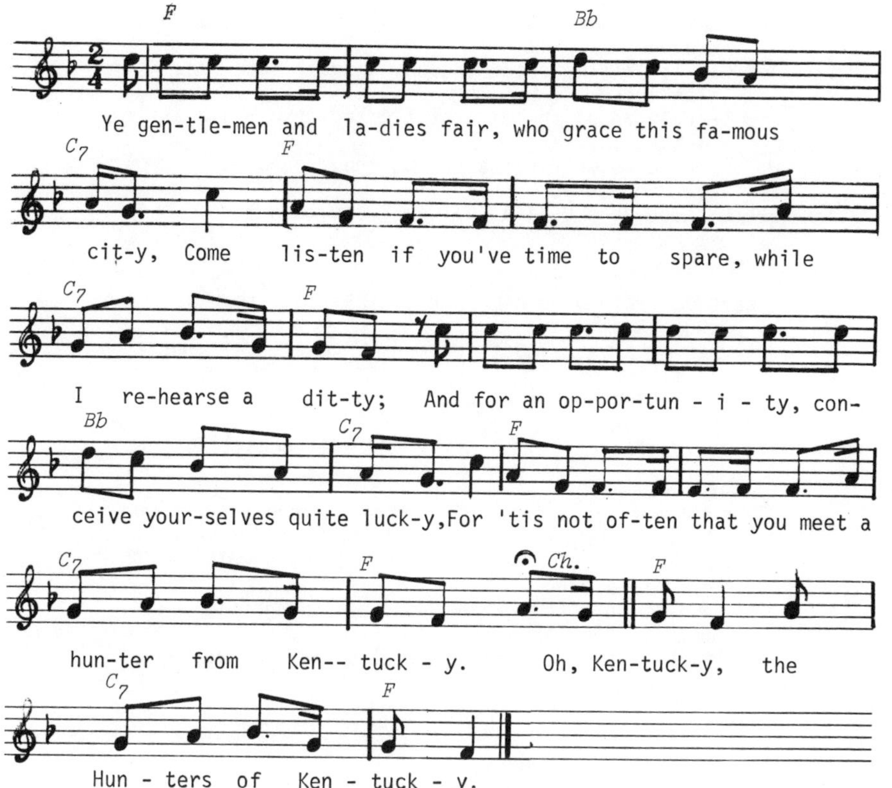

2. I suppose you've read it in the prints, how Packenham attempted
To make Old Hickory Jackson wince, but soon his
schemes repented;
For Jackson, he was wide awake, he was not scared
at trifles,
And well he knew what aim to take with our Kentucky rifles.

(Chorus)

3. Old Packenham, he made his brags, if he in fights was lucky,
He'd have our gals in cotton bags, in spite of Old Kentucky;
And we with rifles ready cocked, thought such occasion lucky,
And quickly round the General flocked, the Hunters of Kentucky.
He led us down to cypress swamp, the ground was low and mucky,
There stood John Bull in martial pomp, and here was Old Kentucky.

4. A bank was raised to hide our breasts, not that we thought of dying,
But then we always shoot from rest, unless the game is flying.
Behind it stood our little force, none wished it to be greater,
For every man was half a horse and half an alligator.

5. They did not let our patience tire, before they showed their faces,
We did not choose to waste our fire, and snugly kept our places.
And when so near to see 'em wink, we thought it time to stop 'em,
And 'twould have done you good, I think, to see Kentuckians drop 'em.

6. They found at last 'twas vain to fight, where lead was all their booty,
And so they wisely took to flight, and left us all our beauty.
And now if danger e'er annoys, remember what our trade is,
Just send for us Kentucky boys, and we'll protect your ladies.

THE FATAL DERBY DAY

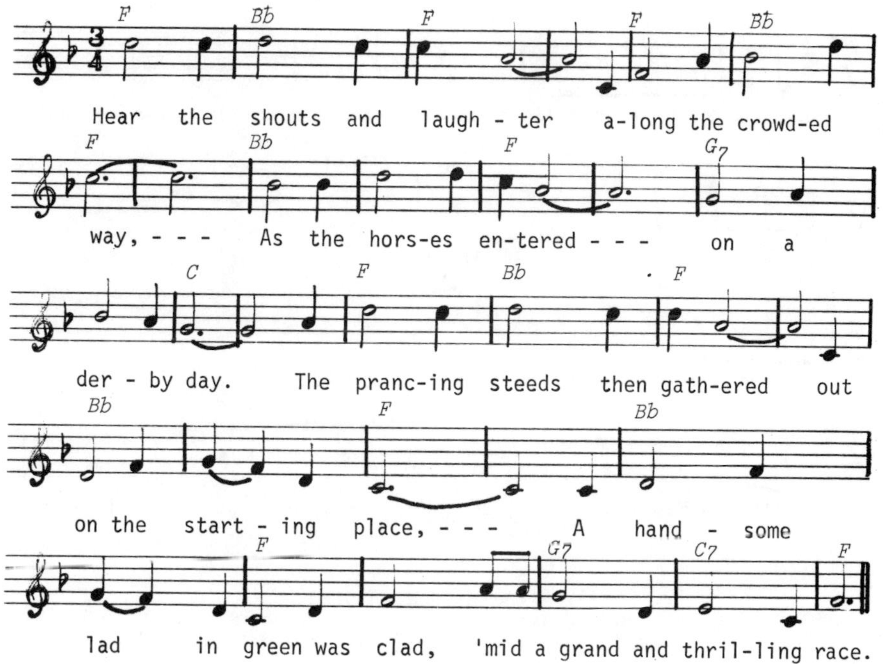

2. Seated in the grandstand, among the gay and glad,
Sat a widowed mother, waiting for her lad.
Soon the race will be over, and as she smiles with joy,
Hoping to see the wreath and prize upon her darling boy.

3. But before the race was over, the leading horse he fell
And crushed the little one beneath his feet, the boy that
she loved so well.
Then was heard the screams for mercy amid this anxious throng,
One racing horse's back was bare, the boy in green was gone.

4. He sleeps now in the little graveyard, with his named carved
on the stone
Where the horse's image, too, is carved, standing there alone.
His master gone forever, no one can take his place,
The bugle blast called him at last to run his fatal race.

5. What greater price, or fortune could a poor widowed mother pay
Than give her boy, her pride and joy, and grieve her life away?
Her faith will not be shaken, for God in all His love
Will give her back her darling boy in a beautiful home above.

OLD NUMBER THREE
(Billy Richardson's Last Ride)

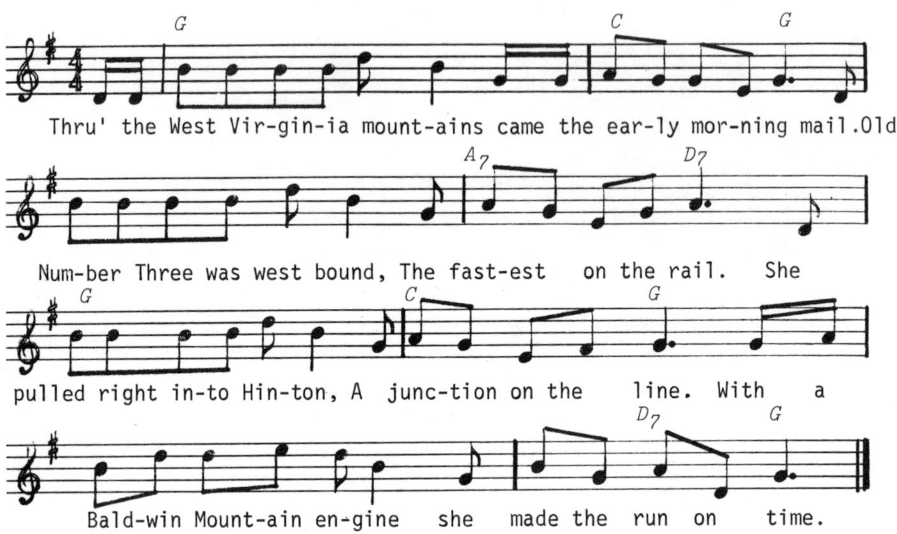

2. Billy Richardson at Hinton,
Was called to take the run,
To pull the fastest mail train
From there to Huntington.
His fireman he reported
For duty on the line.
Then reading their train orders,
Left Hinton right on time.

3. Then Billy told his fireman
That he would happy be,
If he could die while pullin'
A train like Number Three.
"I want to die on duty
Right in my cab," said he,
"While pullin' east bound Number Four
Or west bound Number Three."

4. The fireman then said, "Billy
You know you're old and gray.
Your name is on the pension list.
You should retire some day."
But Billy said, "Dear fireman,
The truth I'm telling you.
I must die right in my engine cab
And nothing else will do."

5. Then pullin' down New River
Came west bound Number Three
By Thurman then by Cottongill,
What danger could it be?
His head then struck the mail train
While pullin' down the line.
He'll never pull his train again
Thru Huntington on time.

6. He pulled the fastest time freight.
He pulled the U.S. Mail.
He pulled a fast excursion
To the music of the rail.
He lost his life on duty
In his engine cab so free,
While pullin' in Montgomery
On west bound Number Three.

7. Now ladies, if your husband
Is a railroad engineer,
You know he is in danger
And death is ever near.
You know he loves you dearly
When he is by your side,
But remember well that his next run
May be his farewell ride.

PEARL BRYAN

2. She died not broken hearted,
Nor from sickness did she fail,
But in one moment parted
From the home she loved so well.

3. Last night the moon shone brightly,
The stars were shining too.
Down to this maiden's cottage,
A jealous lover came.

4. Come, love, and let us wander,
Down to the meadow gate,
And we will wander and ponder,
O'er the coming of our wedding day.

5. The way was cold and dreary,
The night was coming on.
Into this lonely valley
He led this maiden on.

6. "Scott Jackson I am tired,
Of wandering here so long,
The way is cold and dreary,
I pray you take me home."

7. "You have not the wings of an eagle,
Nor from me can you fly
No human hand can aid you,
You instantly must die."

8. "What have I done, Scott Jackson,
That you should take my life?
You know I've always been good to you
And promised to be your wife."

9. Down on her knees before him,
She pleaded for her life,
And into that snowy bosom,
He plunged a gleaming knife.

10. "Scott Jackson, I'll forgive you,
With my last and dying breath,
I never have deceived you,
As I close my eyes in death."

11. Down on his knees he bended,
Saying, "Oh, what have I done?
I've murdered my Pearl Bryan,
As pure as the rising sun."

12. Now in that lonely valley,
Where the willows weep o'er her grave,
Pearl Bryan lies forgotten
Where the merry sunbeams play.

THE TRUE AND TREMBLING BRAKEMAN

2. See those car wheels passing o'er him,
O'er his mangled body and head'
See his sister bending o'er him,
Crying, "Brother, are you dead?"

3. "Dying, sister, yes, I'm dying,
Going to join that better shore;
Oh, my father and my mother,
I shall never see no more."

4. See that brave young engineer
At the age of twenty-one
As he's stepping from his engine,
Crying now, "What have I done?"

5. "Have I killed that faithful brakeman,
Can it be that he is dying?
Oh, I did my best to save him,
But I could not stop in time."

6. "Dying, Buddy, yes I'm dying,
Going to join that better shore;
Oh, my buddy on the T.C.
I shall never see no more."

7. "Sister, when you see my brother,
These few words I send to him;
Never, never, venture braking,
If he does his life will end."

8. These few words that he had spoken,
Clasped his hands across his breast;
For his spirit all had left him,
And his soul had gone to rest.

TWO LITTLE ORPHANS

2. "Mamma's in heaven, they took her away,
Left Jim and I all alone.
We came here to stay, 'til the close of the day
For we have no mamma, no home.
We can't earn our bread, we're too little," she said.
"Jim five years, and I only seven.
No one to love us since papa is dead
And our darling mamma is in heaven."

3. Papa was lost out on the sea long ago,
We waited all night on the shore.
For he was a life-saving captain, you know,
But he never came back any more.
Then mamma got sick, angels took her away,
They said to a home fair and bright.
She said she would come for her darlings some time
Perhaps she is coming tonight."

4. The sexton came early to ring the church bell,
He found them all covered snow white,
The angels made room for two children to dwell
In heaven with mamma tonight.

THE DREAM OF THE MINER'S CHILD

2. I dreamed that the mines were all steaming with fire,
The men all fought for their lives;
Just then the scene changed and the mouth of the mine
Was covered with sweethearts and wives.

(Chorus)

3. Her daddy's been smiling and stroking her face,
Was turning away from her side,
But throwing her small arms around daddy's neck
She gave him a kiss and then cried:

4. Go down to the village and tell all your friends
As sure as the bright stars do shine,
There's something that's going to happen today.
Oh Daddy don't go to the mine.

TWO LITTLE FROGS

2. Another little frog lived in the pool,
   Sing a song, kitty, won't you ki-me-o.
   I think he was a great big fool,
   Sing a song, kitty, won't you ki-me-o.

3. Both little frogs jumped into the well,
   Sing a song, kitty, won't you ki-me-o,
   And to this world they bid farewell,
   Sing a song, kitty, won't you ki-me-o.

   (Chorus)

4. One little frog gave up to drown,
Sing a song, kitty, won't you ki-me-o,
But the other little frog kept swimming around,
Sing a song, kitty, won't you ki-me-o.

5. When morning came one frog was gone,
Sing a song, kitty, won't you ki-me-o,
But the other little frog kept paddling along,
Sing a song, kitty, won't you ki-me-o.

6. Down came the waterbucket, flippity flop,
Sing a song, kitty, won't you ki-me-o,
One frog jumped on and rode to the top.
Sing a song, kitty, won't you ki-me-o.

7. That is the end of this little song,
Sing a song, kitty, won't you ki-me-o.
If the shoe fits you, just put it on,
Sing a song, kitty, won't you ki-me-o.

(Chorus)

I WONDER WHEN I SHALL BE MARRIED

2. I fear that too long I have tarried, have tarried,
have tarried,
I fear that too long I have tarried,
I fear I shall be an old maid.

3. My mother is anxious and worried, and worried,
and worried,
My mother is anxious and worried,
She's two other daughters beside.

4. My shoes have gone to be mended, be mended, be
mended,
My shoes have gone to be mended,
And my petticoat is to be dyed.

5. Oh, say won't it be a great bargain, great bargain,
great bargain,
Oh, say, won't it be a great bargain,
When someone gets married to me.

BURY ME BENEATH THE WILLOW

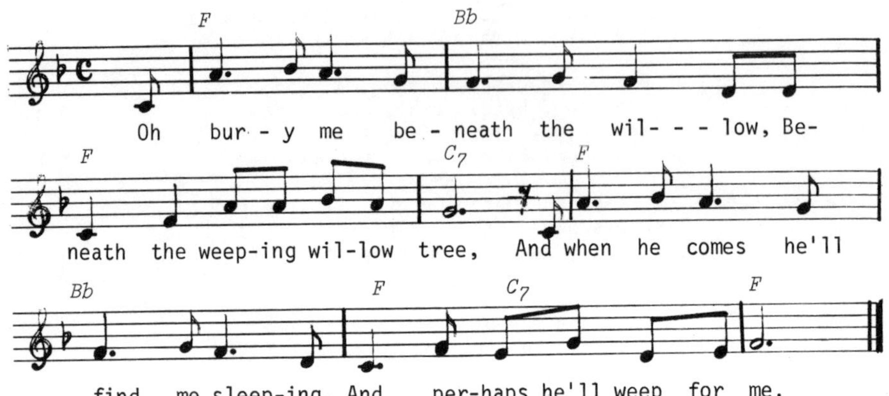

2. Tomorrow was our wedding day,
But now, oh God, my spirit keep.
He's gone, he's gone, to seek another.
He no longer cares for me.

3. My heart's in sorrow, I'm in trouble,
Grieving for the one I love,
For oh, I know I'll never see him,
'Till we meet in Heaven above.

4. They told me that he did not love me,
But how could I believe them true,
Until an angel whispered softly,
He will prove untrue to you.

5. Place on my grave a snow white lily,
For to prove my love to him,
To show the world I died to save him,
But his love I could not win.

6. So bury me beneath the willow,
Beneath the weeping willow tree,
And when he comes he'll find me sleeping,
And perhaps he'll think of me.

THE TRUE LOVER'S FAREWELL

2. Ten thousand miles my own true love,
Ten thousand miles or more.
The rocks may melt and the sea may burn
If I no more return.

3. And who will shoe your feet my love,
And who will glove your hand?
O, who will kiss your red rosy cheek
When I'm in that far off land?

4. My father will shoe my pretty little feet.
My mother will glove my hand,
And you can kiss my red rosy cheek
When you come from the far off land.

5. If I prove false to you my love,
The earth may melt and burn.
The sea may freeze and the earth may burn,
If I no more return.

6. O, don't you see yon little turtle dove
A-skipping from vine to vine,
A-mourning the loss of its own true love,
Just as I mourn for mine?

7. O, don't you see that crow fly high?
She turns both black and white.
If ever I prove false to you
Bright day shall turn to night.

OLD JOE CLARK

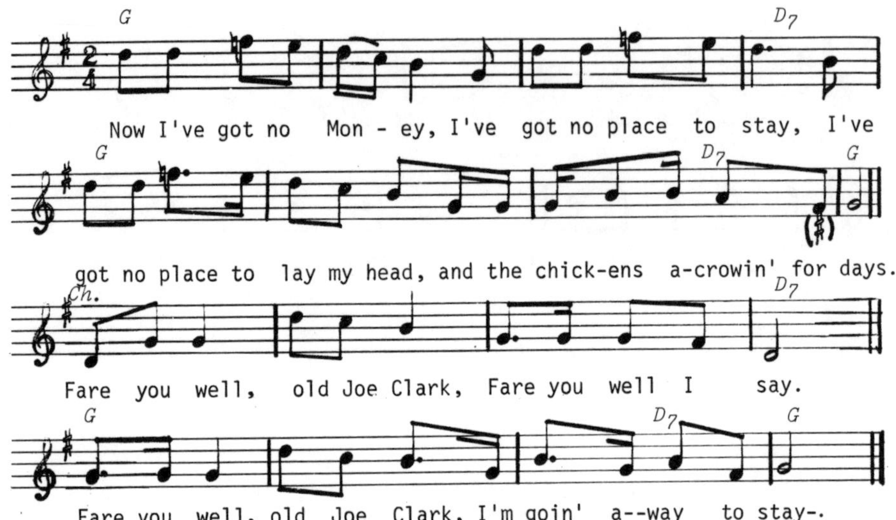

2. I wish I had a nickel,
I wish I had a dime.
I wish I had a pretty little girl
To kiss her and call her mine.

(Chorus)

3. I don't like that old Joe Clark,
I'll tell you the reason why.
He goes about the country
A-stealin' good men's wives.

4. I went down to old Joe Clark's,
I did not mean no harm.
He grabbed his old forty-four
And shot me through the arm.

5. Old Joe Clark's a mean old dog,
I'll tell you the reason why.
He tore down my old rail fence,
So his cattle could eat my rye.

6. I went down to old Joe Clark's,
I found old Joe in bed.
I stuck my finger in old Joe's eye,
And killed old Joe stone dead.

7. I wouldn't marry that old maid,
I'll tell you the reason why.
Her neck's so long and stringy
I'm afraid she'll never die.

8. I went down to Dinah's house,
She was standin' in the door.
With her shoes and stockings in her hand,
And her feet all over the floor.

9. Yonder sits a turtle dove,
Sitting on yonder pine.
You may weep for your true love
And I shall weep for mine.

10. Old Joe Clark's a mighty man.
What will it take to please him?
A good old bottle of apple jack
And Betty Brown to squeeze him.

BURY ME OUT ON THE PRAIRIE

2. My pal was a straight young puncher
Honest and upright and square.
But he turned to a gunman and gambler
And a woman sent him there.
Quicker and surer his gun play,
Till his heart in his body lay dead;
When a vaquero insulted her picture,
He filled him full of lead.

3. All night long they trailed him
Through mesquite and chaparral
And I couldn't but think of the woman
As I saw him pitch and fall.
If she'd been the pal that she should have,
He might have been raising a son
Instead of out there on the prairie
To fall by the ranger's gun.

4. Death's slow sting did not trouble,
His chances for life were too slim;
But where they were puttin' his body
Was all that worried him.
He lifted his head on his elbow,
The blood from his wound flowed red;
He looked at his pals grouped about him
And whispered to them and said:

5. "Oh, bury me out on the prairie
Where the coyotes may howl o'er my grave,
Bury me out on the prairie
And some of my bones please save.
Wrap me up in my blankets
And bury me deep 'neath the ground,
Cover me over with boulders
Of granite huge and round."

6. So they buried him out on the prairie
And the coyotes still howl o'er his grave,
But his soul is now a-restin'
From the unkind cut she gave.
And many a similar puncher
As he rides by that pile of stone
Recalls some similar woman
And envies his moldin' bones.

OL' COON DOG

2. Somebody stole my old coon dog.
I wish they'd bring him back
To run the big hogs over the fence
And the little ones thru the crack.

(Chorus)

3. The devil's on the hillside
Settin' in the sun
Kickin' off back sticks
A havin' him some fun.

4. Turtle in the mill pond
Rootin' in the moss.
Devil's on the hillside
Swearin' he's a hoss.

5. Possum up a 'simmon tree
Raccoon on the ground.
The raccoon said you son of a gun
Shake them 'simmons down.

6. Possum up a gum stump
Raccoon in the holler,
Pretty gal at Massa's house
As fat as she can waller.

7. Massa had an old coon dog
As blind as he could be.
He treed a possum up a black gum stump
I believe that dog could see.

8. Whoa, mule I tell you
Whoa, mule I holler.
Tie a knot in that mule's tail
An' he'll go thru the collar.

9. Watch that mule go roun' the hill,
Watch him how he sails,
Watch him how he shakes his ears
And how he shakes his tail.

FREE A LITTLE BIRD AS I CAN BE

2. Oh, if I was a little honey bee
All out thru the fields I would roam.
I would steal one kiss from my true lover's lips
To sweeten the honey in the comb.

3. If I was a pretty little star
A smiling down on the world,
I would shine my light on my true love tonight
And I'd play on her beautiful curls.

4. I'm as free a little bird as I can be.
I'm as free a little bird as I can be,
Sitting on the roadside a mourning all my days
For nobody cares for me.

I LOVE LITTLE WILLIE

2. He asked me to marry, he did Mama,
He asked me to marry, ha, ha, ha, ha,
He asked me to marry, but don't you tell Pa
For he won't like it you know.

3. He's gone for the license, he has Mama,
He's gone for the license, ha, ha, ha, ha,
He's gone for the license, but don't you tell Pa
For he won't like you know.

4. The preacher is coming, he is Mama,
The preacher is coming, ha, ha, ha, ha,
The preacher is coming, but don't you tell Pa
For he won't like it you know.

5. Oh, now we are married, we are Mama,
Oh, now we are married, ha, ha, ha, ha,
Oh, now we are married, and you can tell Pa
For he can't help it, you know.

PRETTY LITTLE PINK

2. Lor, Lor, my pretty little Pink,
Lor, Lor I say.
Lor, Lor my pretty little Pink
I'm going away to stay.

3. Cheeks as red as a red, red rose,
Her eyes as a diamond brown.
I'm going to see my pretty little miss
Before the sun goes down.

4. Fly around my pretty little Pink
Fly around my daisy.
Fly around my pretty little Pink
You almost drive me crazy.

5. It's rings upon my true love's hands,
Shines so bright like gold.
Gonna' see my pretty little miss
Before it rains or snows.

6. When I was up in the field at work,
I sat down and cried,
Studying about my blue eyed girl,
Thought to my God I'd die.

7. I don't want none of your weevily wheat,
I don't want none of your barley.
Want some flour in a half an hour
To bake a cake for Charley.

8. Fly around my pretty little miss.
Fly around my dandy.
Fly around my pretty little miss.
I don't want none of your candy.

9. Every time I go that road
It looks so dark and cloudy.
Every time I see that girl
I always tell her howdy.

10. Coffee grows on white oak trees,
The river flows with brandy.
Rocks on the hills all covered with gold,
And the girls all sweeter than candy.

11. I'll put my knapsack on my back,
My rifle on my shoulder.
I'll march away to Spartanburg,
And there I'll be a soldier.

12. Charley is a nice young man,
Charley is a dandy.
Every time he goes to town,
He buys the ladies candy.

13. Every time I go that road,
It looks so dark and hazy.
Every time I see that girl
She almost runs me crazy.

14. I asked that girl to marry me
And what did she say?
She said that she would marry me
Before the break of day.

AIN'T WE CRAZY?

2. It was midnight on the ocean, not a street car was in sight
And the sun was shining brightly for it rained all day that night.
'Twas a summer's night in winter and the rain was snowing fast,
A bare-foot boy with shoes on stood sitting in the grass.
It was evening and the rising sun was setting in the west;
The little fishes in the trees were cuddled in their nest.
The rain was pouring down and the sun was shining bright,
And everything that you could see was hidden from your sight.

(Chorus)

3. While the organ peeled potatoes, lard was rendered by the choir,
While the sexton rang the dish rag, someone set the church on fire,
"Holy smoke!" the preacher shouted, in the rain he lost his hair,
Now his head resembles heaven for there's no parting there.
The cows were making cowslips and the bells were ringing wet,
The bumble bees were making bums and smoking cigarettes.
A man slept in the stable and came out a little horse.
He hopped upon his golf sticks and drove all around the course.

4. It was midnight on the ocean, not a horse car was in sight,
As I stepped into a drug store to get myself a light.
The man behind the counter was a woman old and gray,
Who used to peddle doughnuts on the road to Mandalay.
"Good evening sir," she said, her eyes were bright with tears,
As she put her head beneath her feet and stood that way for years.
Her children, six were orphans except one tiny tot,
Who lived in a house across the street above a vacant lot.

AS I WALKED OUT

2. To see them meet, to hear them talk,
And to hear what they had to say,
I wanted to know what was on their minds,
Before I went away.

3. Come sit you down, my own true love,
Come sit you down, said he.
It's been two years and a half or more
Since your face has been shown to me.

4. I will not sit by you, young man,
By you nor no other man,
Nor will I believe his faith or troth,
For he's sworn to many a one.

5. Don't you remember on yonder mountain top,
When we sat side by side,
You promised me you would marry me,
And would be no other man's bride.

6. Oh, when my heart was yours, young man,
And you robbed so rich a nest,
You made me believe by the oaths you swore,
That the sun rose in the West.

7. I will not believe a young man any more,
Let his eyes be blue, black or brown,
Save he were on the top of a high gallows tree,
A-swearing he wished to come down.

8. If I could live just one more year,
And God would give me grace,
I'd buy me a bottle of old moonshine,
To wash my deceitful face.

THE BEST OLD MAN

2. What'd you get me, my good old man?
   What'd you get me, my good old man?
   What'd you get me, my loving little husband,
   The best old man in the world?

   (Spoken) "Got you a dress."

3. What'd you pay for it my good old man?
   (Repeat first line of each verse three times, adding "my loving little husband," on the third line.)

   (Spoken) "A large great big old nickel."

4. A nickel will break you my good old man.

   (Spoken) "Better eat, I guess."

5. What do you want for your supper my good old man?

   (Spoken) "I want some eggs."

6. How many do you want, my good old man?

   (Spoken) "A bushel."

7. A bushel will kill you my good old man.

   (Spoken) "I don't care."

8. Where do you want to be buried, my good old man?

   (Spoken) "Just put me out behind the chimney corner."

9. Soot will black you my good old man.

PRETTY LITTLE DEVILISH MARY

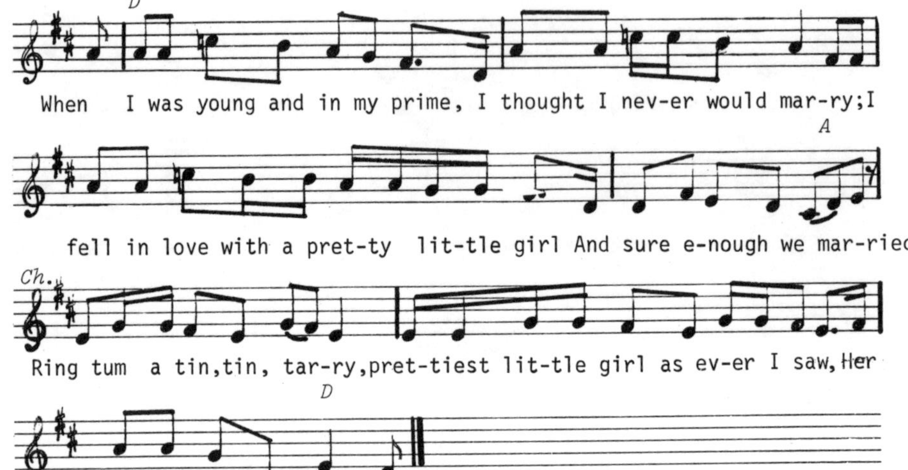

2. We both were young and foolish.
   We got in a mighty big hurry.
   We both agreed on a few little words
   That the weddin' day was Thursday.

   (Chorus)

3. We hadn't been married but about two weeks,
   She got as mean as the devil,
   And every time I looked cross-eyed
   She would knock me on the head with a shovel.

4. She washed my clothes in old soap suds.
   She brushed my back with switches.
   She let me know I had to mind,
   That she was goin' to wear the britches.

5. We hadn't been married but about six months,
   We decided we'd better be parted.
   She up with her little duds
   And down the road she started.

6. If ever I marry the second time,
   It will not be for riches.
   It'll be a little girl about two feet tall,
   So she can't wear my britches.

THE KICKING MULE

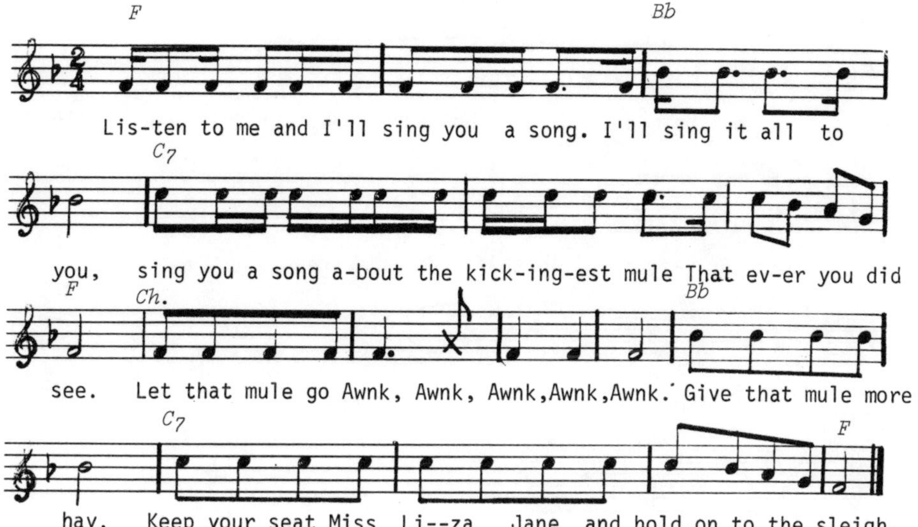

2. Hitched him up early one morning
To take my gal a ride,
Kicked both hind feet over the shaves
And kicked her in the side.

(Chorus)

3. Kicked the wings off of a wild goose
The ears off of a frog,
Kicked the brindle cat upon top of the house
And swallowed a great big dog.

4. Oh, hear them sleigh bells ringing,
The snow is falling fast.
I put this mule in harness
And got him hitched at last.

5. Oh, Liza get your bonnet.
Come and take your seat.
Grab the board you're sitting on,
And kiver up your feet.

6. And watch this mule a climbing,
For this ain't half a load.
Find a mule that's roomy,
And give him all the road.

7. And don't get scared at nothin',
What you hear or see.
Liza, I'll stay with this mule,
And you must stay with me.

8. Just see them snowflakes flying.
Lookout let him sail.
Watch them ears of his'n,
And see him wag his tail.

9. Goin' to the preacher's,
Liza you keep cool.
Hain't got time to kiss you now.
I'm busy with this mule.

10. Little grasshopper came flying around,
Came flying around the well.
This little mule gave him one good kick,
Grasshopper didn't feel so well.

11. Took him down to the blacksmith's shop
Hitched him by himself.
He kicked both hind feet down his neck,
And kicked himself to death.

FOUR THOUSAND YEARS AGO

So you see I'm an educated man,
Keep my brain in my head I plan;
I've been on earth so long,
I used to sing a song,
While Abraham and Isaac rushed the can.

2. I have sat with kings and queens on every hand,
Jack and aces, can't you understand?
And I saw the flags a-flying,
When George Washington stopped lying,
On the night when Patti first began to sing.

3. I saw Eve when she searched that garden o'er.
I saw Satan when they drove him from the door;
While the apples they were eating,
From the bushes I was peeping,
And I'll swear that I'm the man that ate the core.

4. I saw Samson when he laid the village cold.
I saw Daniel tame the lions in the hold;
I helped build the tower of Babel,
Up as high as we were able,
And there's lots of other things I haven't told.

5. I taught Solomon his little ABC's,
I helped Brigham Young to make limburger cheese;
And while sailing down the bay,
With Methuselah one day,
I saved his flowing whiskers from the breeze.

6. Queen Elizabeth she fell in love with me,
We were married in Milwaukee secretly;
But I fooled around and shook her,
And I went with General Hooker,
To shoot mosquitoes down in Tennessee.

7. I remember when the country had a king,
I saw Cleopatra pawn her wedding ring;
I saw Peter, Paul and Moses,
Playing ring around the roses,
I can whip the man that says it isn't so.

THE CUCKOO IS A PRETTY BIRD

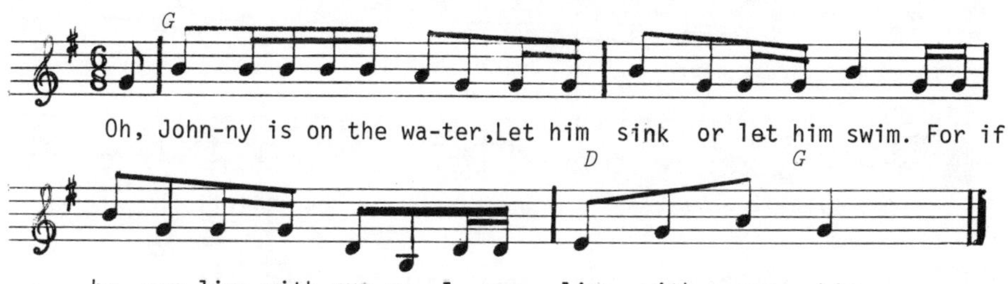

2. Johnny is a young boy,
But still younger am I;
But how often has he told me
He'd wed me or die.

3. O meeting is a pleasure
And parting is grief,
But an unconstant true love
Is worse than a thief.

4. A thief can but rob you
And take all you have,
But an unconstant lover
Will take you to your grave.

5. I'll take off this black dress
And I'll flourish in green,
For I don't care if I'm forsaken
I am only nineteen.
Hiccough, O Lordy, how bad I do feel,
Hiccough, O Lordy, how bad I do feel.

6. The grave it will rot you
And turn you to dust;
There ain't one out of twenty
That a young girl can trust.

7. They will court and kiss you
And get your heart warm,
But as soon as your back's turned
They'll laugh you to scorn.

8. The cuckoo is a pretty bird,
She sings as she flies;
She brings us good tidings
And tells us no lies.

9. Forsaken, forsaken,
Forsaken am I.
He is certainly mistaken
If he thinks that I'll cry.

METHODIST PIE

2. There's old Uncle Daniel
And Brother Ebenezer,
Uncle Rufus with his lame gal, Sue,
Aunt Polly and Melinda
And old Mother Bender
Well, I never seen a happier crew.

3. Well, they all go there
For to have a good time
And to eat that grub so sly.
Have applesauce butter
With sugar in the gourd
And a great big Methodist Pie.

(Chorus)

4. Well, you ought to hear the ringing
When they all get to singing
That good old bye and bye.
See Jimmy McGee in the top of a tree,
Saying, how is this for high?

5. Then they cotch a hold of hands
And march around the ring,
Kept a-singing all the while.
You'd think it was a cyclone
Coming through the air,
You could hear them shout a half a mile.

6. Then the bell rings loud and the great big crowd
Breaks ranks and up they fly.
While I took board
On the sugar in the gourd
And I cleaned up the Methodist Pie.

(Chorus)

GET AWAY, OLD MAN, GET AWAY!

2. I would rather have a young man
With an apple in his hand,
Than ever marry an old man
With all his house and lands.

3. I would rather have a young man,
With his pocket lined with silk,
Than to ever marry an old man
With all his cows to milk.

4. I'll never marry an old man
With his teeth all falling out.
His hand has got the palsy,
His feet has got the gout.

5. The old men come a-grumbling home
And are weary of their life.
A young man comes a-skipping,
Saying, "Kiss me, darling wife."

LIZA UP IN THE 'SIMMON TREE

2. The old folks down in the mountains, grinding sugar cane,
Making barrels of molasses, for to sweeten old Liza Jane.

3. Whiskey by the gallon, sugar by the pound,
A great big bowl to put it in, and Liza to stir it around.

4. I went to see my Liza Jane, she was standing in the door,
Shoes and stockings in her hand and her feet all over the floor.

5. Her head is like a coffee pot, her nose is like the spout,
Her mouth is like an old fireplace with the ashes all raked out.

6. I wouldn't marry a poor girl, I'll tell you the reason why,
She'd have so many poor kinfolks, she'd make my biscuits fly.

7. The hardest work I ever done, was a-brakin' on a train,
The easiest work I ever done, was huggin' little Liza Jane.

OLD DAN TUCKER

2. Old Dan Tucker was a fine old man,
Washed his face with the frying pan,
Combed his head with a wagon wheel
And died with a toothache in his heel.
Get out o' the way for old Dan Tucker.
He's too late to get his supper.

3. Old Dan Tucker had a balky mule,
Hitched him backward as a rule.
When he'd get balky on the road,
He'd back in town with a heavy load.

4. Daniel Tucker's big and fat,
His eyes as black as my old hat,
His mouth sticks out,
His chin caves in,
He's a good lookin' man for the shape he's in.
Get out o' the way, old Dan Tucker.
You come too late to get your supper.

5. Daniel Tucker had a gal named Sue.
She always wore a dress of blue.
Her eyes were brown and her cheeks were red,
And her biscuits were as heavy
As a ton of lead.
Get out o' the way, old Dan Tucker.
You come too late to get your supper.

6. Daniel Tucker came home one night.
His wife accused him of being tight.
Dan got mad and grabbed his gun,
Then Mrs. Tucker left on the run, saying:
Get out o' the way, old Dan Tucker.
You come too late to get your supper.

7. Now Daniel Tucker's dead and gone.
I never saw the like since I've been born.
He left a wife and seventeen children.
He died of old age, you couldn't kill 'im.

GROUND HOG

(Repeat first line of each verse.)

2. Come on boys, let's go down.
We'll catch a whistle pig on this round.

3. Skin that whistle pig put him on to boil.
Bet by the dickens you could smell him a mile.

4. Skin that whistle pig save his hide.
Makes the best shoestring ever I tried.

5. Two little whistle pigs in a pen.
I'll take the hide off of one of them.

6. Up come Vester from the plow.
I want some whistle pig, I want it now.

7. Up come Sal with a snigger and a grin.
Whistle pig grease all over her chin.

DOWN IN THE VALLEY

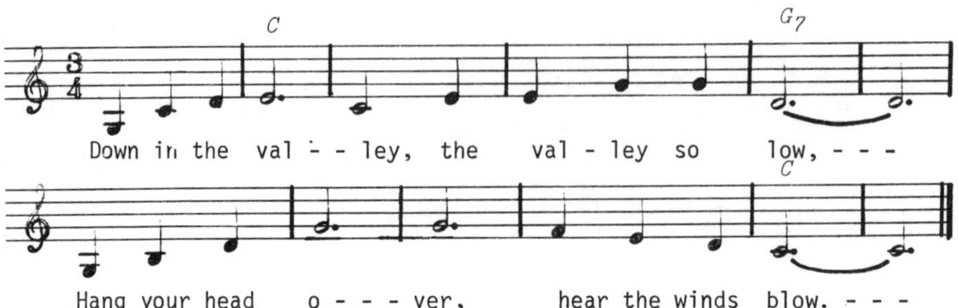

2. If you don't love me, love whom you please,
Throw your arms round me, give my heart ease.
Give my heart ease, dear, give my heart ease.
Throw your arms round me, give my heart ease.

3. Throw your arms round me, before it's too late,
Throw your arms round me, feel my heart break.
Feel my heart break, dear, feel my heart break,
Throw your arms round me, feel my heart break.

4. If you don't love me, none else will do,
My heart is breaking, dear, just for you.
Breaking for you, dear, breaking for you,
My heart is breaking, dear, just for you.

5. Writing this letter containing three lines,
Answer my question, "Will you be mine?"
Will you be mine, dear, will you be mine,
Answer my question, "Will you be mine?"

6. Build me a castle, forty feet high,
So I can see him, as he goes by.
As he goes by, dear, as he goes by,
So I can see him, as he goes by.

7. Down in the valley the mocking bird wings,
Telling my story, here's what he sings:
Roses love sunshine, violets love dew,
Angels in heaven know I love you.
Knows I love you, dear, knows I love you,
Angels in heaven know I love you.

HOME SWEET HOME

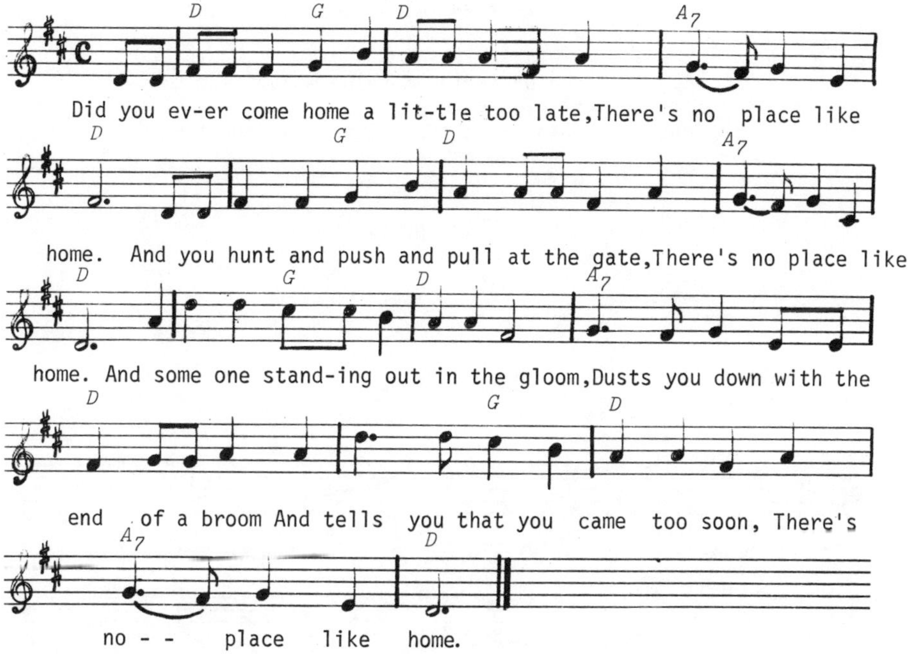

2. When the baby gets the colic in the
 middle of the night,
 There's no place like home.
 And you hunt for paregoric without a light,
 There's no place like home.
 And you step on the point of an upturned tack
 And you yell and holler till your face is blue
 and black,
 And your wife says,"For goodness sake, shut
 up, Jack."
 There's no place like home.

3. When the relatives come to visit you
 There's no place like home.
 They bring all their trunks and stick like glue,
 There's no place like home.
 And you give them the very best bed in the lot,
 While you sleep in the hall on a dirty little cot,
 With your brother-in-law who's about half shot.
 There's no place like home.

4. When the wind begins to whistle and the air is full of snow,
There's no place like home.
And the furnace fire is out and it's twenty-two below,
There's no place like home.
And you wake up in the morning when the clock is striking nine,
And the babies want their breakfast and they all begin to whine,
And your wife's cold feet are in the middle of your spine,
There's no place like home.

TWENTY YEARS AGO

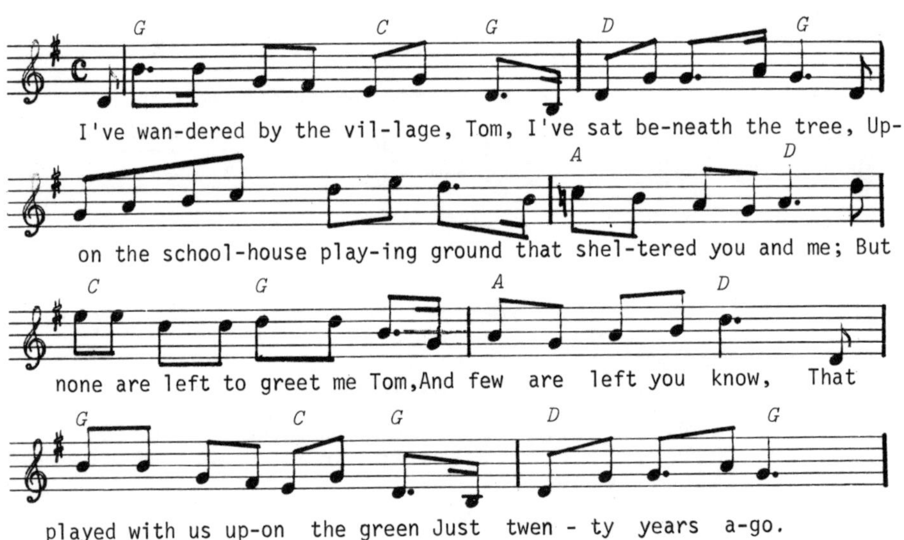

2. The grass is just as green, dear Tom,
Barefooted boys at play
Are sporting just as we were then,
With spirits just as gay;
But master sleeps upon the hill,
All coated o'er with snow.
That offered us a sliding place
Just twenty years ago.

3. The old school house is altered some,
The benches are replaced,
But new ones very like the same,
Our penknives had defaced;
But the same old bricks are in the wall,
The bell swings to and fro,
The music is just the same, dear Tom,
'Twas twenty years ago.

4. The boys are playing some old game,
Beneath the same old tree,
I do forget the name just now,
You've played the same with me;
On that same spot 'twas played with knives,
By throwing so and so,
The leaders had a task to do there
Twenty years ago.

5. The river's running just as still,
The willows on its side
Are larger than they were, dear Tom,
The stream appears less wide;
The grapevine swing is ruined now,
Where once we played the beau
And swung our sweethearts - pretty girls -
Just twenty years ago.

6. The spring that bubbled 'neath the hill,
Close by the spreading beech,
Is very high, 'twas once so low
That we could almost reach;
But in kneeling down to get a drink,
Dear Tom, I started so
To see how sadly I am changed
Since twenty years ago.

LITTLE ROSEWOOD CASKET

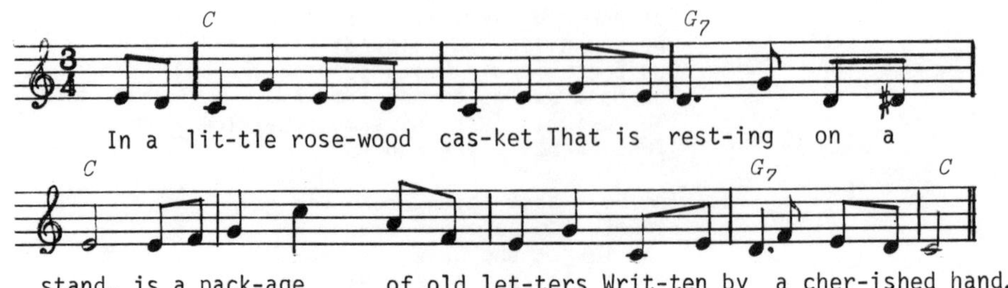

2. Will you go and get them, Sister,
And read them o'er tonight,
For I've oftimes tried, but could not,
For the tears would blind my sight.

3. Read those precious lines so slowly
That I'll not miss even one,
For the precious hand that wrote them,
His last work for me is done.

4. You have got them now, dear Sister,
Come, sit down upon my bed,
And press gently to your bosom
This poor throbbing, aching head.

5. Tell him that I never blamed him,
Not an unkind word was spoke,
Tell, oh, tell him, Sister, tell him,
That my heart in coldness broke.

6. Tell him that I never blamed him,
Though to me he's proved untrue.
Tell him that I'll ne'er forget him
Till I bid this world adieu.

7. When I'm dead and in my coffin,
And my shroud's around me bound,
And my little bed is ready
In the cold and silent ground.

8. Place his letters and his locket
Both together o'er my heart,
But the little ring he gave me
From my finger never part.

9. You have finished, now, dear Sister,
Will you read them o'er again.
While I listen to you read them
I will lose all sense of pain.

10. While I listen to you read them
I will gently fall asleep,
Fall asleep to walk with Jesus,
Oh, dear Sister, do not weep.

I'LL BE ALL SMILES TONIGHT

2. And when the room he entered the bride upon his arm,
I stood and gazed upon him, as if he were a charm.
So once he smiled upon her, so once he smiled on me,
They know not what I suffered, they found no change in me.

(Chorus)

3. And when the dance commences, oh, how I will rejoice,
I'll sing the song he taught me, without one faltering voice.
When flatterers come around me, they will think my heart is light.
Tho my heart will break tomorrow, I'll be all smiles tonight.

4. And when the dance is over, and all have gone to rest,
I'll think of him, dear mother, the one that I love best.
He once did love me dearly, and ne'er would from me part.
He sought not to deceive me, false friends have changed his heart.

THERE'S A RED LIGHT AHEAD

By Bradley Kincaid

As you trav-el down the high-way, my dear broth-er, Go-ing
six-ty miles an hour or more to-day. You may find that you will
not be here to - mor-row, If you do not heed the signs a-long the
way. There's a red light a-head of you dear broth-er, And it's
tel-ling you be care-ful what you do. For you may be called too
soon to face your ma-ker, - - If you do not heed that red light
fac-ing you.

2. Do not wait till it's too late to change, my brother;
Satan's stronghold down below is calling you.
You will never reach those pearly gates up yonder,
If you do not heed that red light facing you.

3. We are told that there will be a resurrection,
And God's chosen ones will start their lives anew.
Do you think that you will rise on that bright morning,
If you do not heed that red light facing you?

4. Have you heard the blessed news about our Saviour?
He is coming to redeem his chosen few.
If you want to live with him in that bright mansion,
Better stop and heed that red light facing you.

THE LEGEND OF THE ROBIN'S RED BREAST

By Bradley Kincaid and Blanche Preston Jones

Oh have you heard this sto--ry it hap-pened long a - go. When
Christ our bless-ed Sa-vior was here on earth be - low, an
ech-o thru the a - ges from dis - tant Cal - va-ry. I'll
tell it to you sim-ply as it was told to me.

Ch. It breathes the bles-sed teach-ing of God's own ho-ly word, A
les-son taught in meek-ness by a low-ly lit-tle bird.

2. When Jesus hung in sorrow our debt of shame to pay,
No one was there to comfort or wipe his tears away.
A little bird flew near him in sober coat of brown
And gazed in tender pity then slowly fluttered down.

3. With gentle wings it fanned him to cool his aching head
And hovered near his bosom all stained with deepest red.
At last when all was ended as if to mourn his loss,
It rose with blood stained feathers and circled 'round the cross.

4. It flew away in sadness and to this day tis said
It wears upon its bosom that stain of crimson red.
When I shall cross the valley and go to seek my rest
May I wear like the robin God's sign upon my breast.

APPENDIX A

A Checklist of Bradley Kincaid's Song Repertory

(See also addendum following checklist)

Note: The following list of songs was compiled from Bradley Kincaid's songbooks, two looseleaf notebooks and recordings, as well as from interviews conducted by this writer and by Archie Green and Eugene Earle with Bradley. Additional information was contributed by D. K. Wilgus. Norm Cohen has added brief annotations, giving either the author/composer and date of composition, or a reference to a standard folk song collection that includes the given item. Comments enclosed in quotation marks are from Bradley. Comments supplied by D. K. Wilgus are followed by his initials. Full bibliographic information on references cited by Norm Cohen is listed below.

Brown — *The Frank C. Brown Collection of North Carolina Folklore*, Vol. 3, ed. Henry M. Belden (Durham: Duke University Press, 1952)

Child — Francis James Child, *The English and Scottish Popular Ballads* (cited by ballad number only)

Laws — G. Malcolm Laws, *Native American Balladry* (Philadelphia: American Folklore Society, 1964); and *American Balladry From British Broadsides* (Philadelphia: American Folklore Society, 1957) (cited by ballad number only; A through I in Native . . . ; J through Q in . . . British . . .)

Randolph — Vance Randolph & Floyd C. Shoemaker, *Ozark Folksongs* (Columbia: State Historical Society of Missouri, 1946-50)

Roberts — Leonard Roberts, *Sang Branch Settlers* (Austin: University of Texas Press for the AFS, 1974)

Sharp — Cecil J. Sharp & Maud Karpeles, *English Folk-Songs from the Southern Appalachians*, Vol. 2 (London: Oxford Univ. Press, 1932)

Sharp (1908) — Cecil J. Sharp, *Folk Songs from Somerset*, 4th series (London: 1908)

Lomax — John A. Lomax and Alan Lomax, *Cowboy Songs and other Frontier Ballads* (NY: Macmillan, 1938)

The major portion of this checklist was published in the Winter 1976 issue of the *JEMF Quarterly*.

ABDULLA BULBUL AMIR "Of course that's Russian. I got that from one of those published songbooks. I don't know whose it was, but I remember getting it out of a big book. That's all I can tell you about it." (Published by Frank Crumit, 1928, but based on an older song)

AFTER THE BALL "A published song. I learned that from my father. I only used the verses. I never used the chorus, but it told quite a story." (by Chas. K. Harris, 1892)

AIN'T WE CRAZY? "I learned from a couple of boys who used to sing it on WLS. That was back in 1927." Hiram and Henry Hornsby (Steve Cisler) (Recorded by Harry McClintock in Sept. 1928)

ALICE BLUE GOWN "A popular song of the thirties which I occasionally used in radio." (by Harry Tierney)

ALL I DO IS DREAM THE WHOLE DAY THROUGH (by Herb Brown, 1934)

THE ANGELS IN HEAVEN KNOW I LOVE YOU "That is 'Down in the

Valley'–an old ballad. I learned that in Berea, believe it or not, I think from Gladys Jameson." (Randolph IV, 284)

AND SO YOU HAVE COME BACK TO ME "I learned from an aunt who is now in her 80's–lives up in Eastern Kentucky–Mrs. Stanley Maxwell."

ARKANSAS TRAVELER "Plain old fiddle tune. I found a collection of words somewhere. I don't know where."

AS I WALKED OUT "Very old song. My mother used to sing it when I was a boy, and I have no idea of the origin."

AWAY SHE WENT GALLOPING DOWN THE LONG LANE "I learned that from my father. He learned it from his folks, so that is a traditional one."

THE BAND PLAYED ON "A published song. I got that from the Southern Music Publishing Company's book. Not mine but one they had published." (by Chas. B. Ward & John F. Palmer, 1895)

BARBARA ALLEN "Sang at home, but in doing research I found Barbara Allen in a collection of old folk songs at a Chicago library–not folk songs but Scotch poems that was dated 500 years back. It was in the old English Shakespearean type spelling." Brad indicated that although he had heard it sung by many, he recalls learning it from his uncle Ben Kincaid. (DKW) (Child No. 84)

BARNEY MCCOY "An old Irish number that goes back to about 1850 or 60." He does not recall having seen it in print. (DKW) (Larry Miller, wds., J. D. Murphy, mus., 1881, however, there may be an older version)

THE BEAUTIFUL CAVERNS OF LURAY "Somebody sent me the words and I put a tune to it. There has been another song published, and I think it is called 'The Caverns of Luray' that has an entirely different tune."

BEAUTIFUL DREAMER "Of course you know who wrote that–Stephen Foster. A published song." (by S. Foster, 1864)

BEAUTIFUL ISLE OF SOMEWHERE "An old hymn that I have known for years and years and years. I don't know what its origin is or whether it was in public domain. I guess it is but I don't know much about it. I found it in a songbook." (Jessie B. Pounds, wds., John S. Fearis, mus., 1897)

BEAUTIFUL OHIO "A popular song of the thirties, which was the theme song used in a program fed to NBC from WLW, in which I participated." (by Ballard MacDonald and Robert A. King, 1918)

THE BEST OLD MAN "Another one I learned from my family." (Randolph III, 173)

BETTY BROWN " 'Betty Brown' is one I learned from Scott Wiseman."

BIBLE STORIES "A 'would be' comedy song based on strict biblical requirements concerning personal conduct in the early days of the Baptist Church. A line in the chorus 'Join the Baptist Sunday School and make yourself at home.' "

BICYCLE BUILT FOR TWO "A popular song used occasionally." (by Harry Dacree, 1936)

BIG ROCK CANDY MOUNTAIN "It was popular during the 1930's. I took it from a Burl Ives collection."

BILLY BOY "An old traditional song. You'll find it in practically any collection. Learned it from a collection." (Randolph I, 393)

BLACK EYED GAL "The next two, 'Black Eyed Gal' and 'Black Eyed Susie' are old fiddle tunes. I found words in some collection someplace and used to sing them."

BLACK EYED SUSIE "Old fiddle tune."

THE BLIND CHILD "And 'The Blind Girl' are old songs that I picked up and I can't tell you where. They are two different songs."

THE BLIND GIRL See "The Blind Child." He recalled learning it from his family. (DKW) (Randolph IV, 191)

BLUE EYES "Old and popular mountain song which I used regularly."

THE BLUE JUNIATA "A little Indian song that somebody sent me in 1928. The notes were written down and had been passed on to them. Whoever sent it had never seen sheet music or anything for it. I learned it and sang it on the air all the time I was in radio . . . A great many of the songs I had in my collection were sent to me. (by Marion D. Sullivan, 1844)

THE BLUE TAIL FLY "I found that in a collection of old songs dated in, I think, 1840. This was simply a minstrel song." (by Dan Emmett?, 1846)

BONAPARTE'S RETREAT "A popular song written by Redd Stewart who worked with Pee Wee King. Redd also wrote 'Tennessee Waltz.' " (with Pee Wee King)

BOYS KEEP AWAY FROM THE GIRLS, I SAY "The correct title is 'The Baldheaded End of a Broom.' One of a number of songs I learned from Doc Hopkins."

BRUSH THE DUST FROM THAT OLD BIBLE "I wrote myself, both words and music. I thought that would be a big hit, but it refers to the bombs and I don't know, people might have been afraid of it."

BURY ME BENEATH THE WILLOW "Another traditional song. You'll find it in most collections. Got it from a collection." (Randolph IV, 228)

BURY ME OUT ON THE PRAIRIE "Learned from a record made by Carson Robison and Vernon Dalhart." (Lomax, 300)

THE BUTCHER BOY (I Died For Love) "Found in a collection." (Laws P 24)

CAPTAIN BILL Composed by Bradley in 1940s.

CARELESS LOVE "Found in a collection." (Randolph IV, 306)

THE CAT CAME BACK "I found in a collection; it's a little comedy song." (by H. S. Miller, 1893)

CHARLES GITEAU AND JAMES A. GARFIELD "A true ballad. Charles Giteau murdered President James A. Garfield. It was popular when I was a boy." (Brown II, 572ff.)

CHARLIE BROOKS "Another one of those love songs of a broken heart and all that sort of thing. I don't know where I learned it." Learned from a cousin. (DKW) (Randolph IV, 210)

THE CHARMING YOUNG WIDOW I MET ON THE TRAIN "Is a published song of early origin. I used to like it. It tells a very interesting story of how the young widow left the young gentleman with a baby, and she never did come back." (Based on song by W. H. Cove, 1868)

CHEWING GUM "I heard that from some little cowgirl someplace. I can't give you much on that."

CINDY "I learned from Scotty Wiseman when Dean Edwards from Berea and I went on a trip down through the mountains. I was collecting old ballads." (Brown III, 482)

COLLECTING PARSON "I learned this fifty years ago from King Owen, a boy working in a tent show with me. I've never seen it written or performed anywhere else." (a poem or talking song)

COME ALL YOU FAIR AND TENDER LADIES "A traditional folk song which I learned from Gladys Jameson at Berea." (Brown III, 290ff.)

CORNPONE AND MOLASSES (Composed by Bradley Kincaid)

COWBOY'S DREAM "Written by Bob Miller in the thirties. It is also called 'Roll On, Little Doggies.' "

THE CRADLE AND THE MUSIC BOX "Popular song of the thirties."

THE CRAWDAD SONG "Old time, so-called 'Hillbilly' song. Popular with old time fiddlers."

CUCKOO IS A PRETTY BIRD (A Forsaken Lover) "My folks used to sing it—my father." (Randolph I, 239)

DADDY AND HOME "One of Jimmie Rodgers' songs. I got that off of one of his records." (by Elsie McWilliams and Jimmie Rodgers, 1929)

THE DAME I LEFT BEHIND ME "That's an old fiddle tune." (The Girl I Left Behind Me.)

DARBY'S RAM "I learned from Grandpa Jones." Learned about 1922. (DKW) (Randolph I, 398)

DARLING CLEMENTINE "Of course everybody knows the history of that." (by Percy Montrose, 1884)

DARLING CORY "Is a very old mountain song that I learned from my brother-in-law, Dr. John Baker, who lived in Berea, Kentucky. He was from way up around Manchester, Ky. in the eastern part of the state." (Roberts, 154)

DARLING NELLIE GRAY "An old one that everybody knows. That's an old plantation song." (by B. R. Hanby, 1856)
DE LADIES' MAN "Was given to me by Professor John Smith when I was a student at Berea, Kentucky. He was sort of a collector of folk songs."
DEAR OLD GIRL "Early 1900 published song. Very popular with Barber Shop Quartets." (by Richard Henry Buck and Theodore Morse, 1903)
THE DEATH OF JIMMIE RODGERS " 'The Death of Jimmie Rodgers' and also 'The Life of Jimmie Rodgers,' were two songs I wrote the tunes for. Bob Miller was publisher in New York, and he came over to Victor Studios one day when I was doing recordings, and he had these words–Jimmie had just died–and he had no tunes. So, I sat down and fooled with it for a little while, and pretty soon I made up a tune, and we recorded it, and the same way with 'The Life of Jimmie Rodgers.' "
DINAH "A very old number that I found in some collection somewhere . . . my father used to sing the tune."
DON'T MAKE ME GO TO BED AND I'LL BE GOOD "A song that Hugh Cross, who has now gone to his reward, claimed that he wrote. Roy Acuff did that too. I don't know if he [Roy] contributed anything to the verses or not, but he certainly sings it pathetically if you know what I mean." (by H. Cross, 19 ?)
DON'T YOU FEEL SORRY FOR MAGGIE? "One of those old songs I learned from my Aunt Stanley Maxwell in Clay City, Kentucky, about forty or fifty years ago. I don't know its origin.
DOG AND GUN "I learned from my father." (Laws N 20)
DOWN BY THE RAILROAD TRACK "I learned from Jack Foy, who used to be a member of the team of Jack and Jerry Foy at WLW and at Schenectady." (by Frank Crumit and Billy Curtis)
DOWN ON THE OLD PLANTATION "A song that was, I believe, written by Carson Robison. I'm pretty sure he wrote that." (by C. Robison, ca 1930)
THE DREAM OF THE MINER'S CHILD "I learned from a little boy sitting with an old beat-up guitar when I was playing a theatre–I think it was Corbin or one of those mining towns in east Kentucky." He learned it between 1929-31. (DKW) (originally "Don't Go Down in the Mines, Dad," by Robert Donnelley & Will Geddes, 1910). For an intriguing exploration of the relationship between "The Dream of a Miner's Child" and "Don't Go Down in the Mines, Dad," see Archie Green's *Only A Miner* (Urbana: University of Illinois Press, 1972), pp. 113-154.
DYING COWBOY "I have sung that ever since I first started singing folk songs. It was one of those songs that was prevalent out in the country where I was raised, and that's about all I can tell you about that." (Laws

B 1) (See also comments under "Streets of Laredo")

EBENEZER FRYE "If there ever was a 'hillbilly' song, this is it. I don't know its origin."

EVERYTHING IS PEACHES DOWN IN GEORGIA "A published song, used and made popular for a time by Clayton McMitchen." (by Milton Ager and George W. Meyer)

FAIR ELLEN "I learned from my mother." (Child No. 73)

FAREWELL LOVELY POLLY "Another one of those that came out of the collections I found." From early Kentucky folk song collection. (DKW) (Laws 0 39)

FAREWELL MY DARLING "A soldier song of the Civil War type."

FARTHER ALONG "An old hymn that Grandpa Jones used to sing when he was on my program. You could say that I learned it from him. It was in one of these old hymn books, and that was his favorite hymn."

THE FATAL DERBY DAY "I got that from Doc Hopkins. The story behind it is the Derby at Louisville. There was an old blind man by the name of Dick Cox that used to go from Louisville to Junction City with his fiddle and tin cup and play his fiddle on the train and take up a collection. He wrote the song of the little boy whose horse fell and killed him. His mother was sitting in the grandstand and saw it–a pretty sad affair. This blind man, according to Doc [Hopkins] wrote this song." Brad told me the same story. However, Doc Hopkins states that he learned the song as "The Little Boy in Green" from Boone Stout in his medicine show days and recomposed it into the form he passed on to Brad. Doc never attributed it to Dick Cox, and the other information I have points to a pop song origin. (DKW)

FATAL ROSE OF RED "One of those published songs that tells a story of misunderstood love." (by Ed Gardenier & J. Fred Helf, 1900)

A FATAL WEDDING "I learned that from my father. It was a published song." (W.H. Windom, wds., Gussie Davis, mus., 1893)

THE FATE OF JOHN HENRY LEE "The words were sent to me by Blanche Preston Jones of Ashland, Kentucky. I put a tune to it."

FATHER GRUMBLE "Found in a collection." From an early Kentucky folk song collection. (DKW) (Randolph I, 318)

FATHER, TELL ME WHAT'S THE ANSWER "Written by yours truly, but I could never get it just right tunewise." (by Bradley Kincaid)

FIFTY YEARS FROM NOW "I wrote the tune. Someone sent me the words." (This appeared in Kincaid's 5th songbook, published in 1932. Harry McClintock recorded the same words in Oct. 1931.)

FINGERPRINTS UPON THE WINDOW PANE "I learned that when I had a tent show some years ago out of Rochester, N. Y. I was working then. I had a cowboy act–one fellow that was a single act–and that was his candy stick. He used to sing 'Fingerprints Upon the Window Pane' and they always liked it."

THE FIRST WHIPPOORWILL'S SONG "I learned from Scott Wiseman."

THE FOGGY DEW* "Found in a collection." Found in a book of about 1840–but I suspect it came to Brad at the session he did for Kapp, set up for the Irish Market, see 'That Tumble Down Shack in Athlone.' (Because the song is a lyric, my files cannot provide immediately Irish references, though it gave rise to some narrative songs. It does occur in a number of early Irish collections. I know it is in the Bunting Collection–but can't recall if any of the text is given. I'm sure I have one or more commercial recordings (78's) of it.) (It is not, of course, the "Bugaboo" item.) (DKW)

FOND OF CHEWING GUM "I don't know where I got the tune, but I made up most of the words to it."

FOOTPRINTS IN THE SNOW "That I can't tell you too much about. I just know it's old. Learned about 1929 or 30." (by Boyd Lane, 1947)

FOR SALE A BABY "A published song. One of those early ones, and I can remember how pitiful it sounded." (by Chas. K. Harris, 1903)

FOUR THOUSAND YEARS AGO "A real old one. I don't know–I heard that when I was at WLS in Chicago. I wouldn't be surprised if it wasn't published, though I never saw it in published form. A very silly song." Contrary to his later statement, Brad told me it was a "family song." (DKW) (Randolph III, 144)

FRANKIE (Gambler's Song) "Of course everybody knows 'Frankie and Johnny.' There are many variations of that. It even gets mixed up with 'John Henry' in some of its arrangements." (Laws I 3)

FREE A LITTLE BIRD AS I CAN BE "I learned from Doc Hopkins. He used to be on WLW and played a nice guitar. He played several of these songs." (Brown III, 296)

FROGGIE WENT A-COURTIN' "I learned from my mother." (Randolph I, 402)

GALLANT AND GAY "One of those old Irish songs that I learned from my father." (Laws P 3)

GET AWAY, OLD MAN, GET AWAY "Everybody knows. Just learned it from hearing it." (by Frank Crumit, 1927)

THE GIRL I LEFT BEHIND ME "Everybody knows. Learned it from hearing it."

GIRL I LOVED IN SUNNY TENNESSEE "Published in the 80's." (by Harry Braisted)

GIVE MY LOVE TO NELL "I never saw it in published style, but I've always felt that it was a published song." He also identified this as a family

song. (DKW) (by Wm. B. Grey, 1894)
GOOSEBERRY PIE "Learned from Doc Hopkins."
GRANDFATHER'S CLOCK (by Henry Clay Work, 1876)
GRANNY ONLY LEFT TO ME HER OLD ARM CHAIR "I've been singing from the very beginning. I honestly don't know where I got it." ("The Old Arm Chair," by Henry Russell, 1840)
GROUND HOG "Old traditional song." (Randolph III, 150)
THE GYPSIE LADDIE "Old traditional one." (Child No. 200)
THE GYPSY'S WARNING "Old traditional one." (by Henry A. Coard, 1864)
HAPPY DAYS LONG AGO "Found in a collection." A parody of "Long, Long Ago." (DKW)
HAVE I TOLD YOU LATELY? (by Scott Wiseman, 1945. First recorded by Gene Autry)
HIGH GRASS TOWN "I learned right here in Berea from a little boy up in the mountains here. I think he was from up around Hazard. He was in a wheelchair very much crippled up, but he was a bright and smart little boy. He used to sit in that wheelchair and he had a guitar and he would just sing up a storm. Can't remember his name."
THE HILLS OF OLD NEW HAMPSHIRE "A published song by Southern Music. Father used to sing that. One of the first published songs." (Originally "My Old New Hampshire House," by Harry Von Tilzer & Andrew B. Sterling, 1898)
HOME ON THE RANGE "Came into being for me when I was at WLS. When I first started in radio business 'Home On the Range' was one of the songs that the cowboys were bringing in." (Brewster Higley, wds., Daniel E. Kelley, mus., 1876)
HOME SWEET HOME "Learned from George Campbell who used to direct a quartet in which I sang tenor when I was in college in Chicago." (John H. Payne, wds., & Henry R. Bishop, mus., 182?)
THE HOUSE CARPENTER "Old traditional one. Found in a collection." (Child No. 243)
THE HOUSE AT THE END OF THE LANE "I learned this from Grandpa Jones in the early thirties. I know nothing of its origin."
A HOUSEKEEPERS TRAGEDY "Somebody sent it to me." (Brown III, 367)
HOW BEAUTIFUL HEAVEN MUST BE "Another hymn like some of the others we've mentioned here that I got out of a songbook. It was popular with Asher and Little Jimmie Sizemore in the 1930's." (by Mrs. A. S. Bridgewater & A. P. Bland, 19 ?)
HOW THE BANJO WAS INVENTED "I believe I got that from my father.

This was sort of a minstrel song—a comedy song."

HUMMINGBIRD SPECIAL "I wrote words and music when I was at Nashville at Grand Ole Opry."

THE HUNTERS OF KENTUCKY "Goes back to the Battle of 1815 in New Orleans." (by Samuel Woodworth, 1812)

I AM THINKING TONIGHT OF MY BLUE EYES

I'M SAVING UP COUPONS TO GET ONE OF THOSE "A comedy song I heard a comedian sing at WLW. Never very popular."

I ASKED HER IF SHE LOVED ME (Over There) "One of my father's old songs."

I COULD NOT CALL HER MOTHER "Traditional song that came along. I don't know origin." Brad identified this as a song from his family. (DKW) (At least 2 copyrighted versions: Sarah T. Bolton, wds., R. Sinclair, mus., 1854; and by Harry Harrison, 1855)

I GAVE MY LOVE A CHERRY "One of my father's songs." (Sharp II, 190)

I HAD BUT FIFTY CENTS "A comedy song published by Jerry Vogel Music Co. in the thirties. I never used it."

I LOVE LITTLE WILLIE "One of my father's songs." (Randolph III, 198)

I LOVE MY ROOSTER "I wrote most of the words when I was in Berea in school."

I LOVED YOU BETTER THAN YOU KNEW "I got from my Aunt Stanley." (cf. Randolph IV, 215)

I MISS MY SWISS "A good yodeling song sung by most of the best yodeling cowgirls in the 40's and 50's." (by L. Wolfe Gilbert and Abel Baer, 1925)

I WONDER WHEN I SHALL BE MARRIED "One of my father's songs."

I WON'T BE BACK IN A YEAR, LITTLE DARLING (Composed by Bradley in 1940s)

I'D LIKE TO BE IN TEXAS "Found in a collection."

I'LL BE ALL SMILES TONIGHT "Traditional song that came along. I don't know origin. Learned from Aunt Stanley, father's sister." (by T. B. Ransom, 1879)

I'LL NEVER KISS YOU ANYMORE "A song published in the late eighties or early nineties. My father sang it. I never used it on the radio."

I'LL REMEMBER YOU, LOVE, IN MY PRAYERS "Learned from my father. Very popular with me on radio." (by Will S. Hays, 1869)

I'LL TAKE YOU HOME AGAIN KATHLEEN "Learned from my father." (by Thos. P. Westendorf, 1876)

I'M DYING FOR SOMEONE TO LOVE ME "Learned from father."

IN THE VALLEY OF KENTUCKY "A popular published song of the

early nineties. It was sung by my father without accompaniment."

I WISH I HAD SOMEONE TO LOVE ME "I wrote words and music."

IF I WAS AS YOUNG AS I USED TO BE "Found in collection."

IN A VILLAGE BY THE SEA "Another one of those disappointed-in-love things where she dies of a broken heart because he went away, and when he came back to see her her father took him down to the graveyard and showed him the grave. I would say that it was at one time published a long, long time ago." (cf. Randolph IV, 321)

IN THE HILLS OF (OLD) KENTUCKY "Was my theme song all during the years. Was published by Forester in Chicago."

IN THE SHADE OF THE OLD APPLE TREE (by Harry Williams and Egbert Van Alstyne, 1905)

IN THE SHADOW OF THE PINE (by Hattie Lummis and G. O. Lang, 1895)

(IN) THE LITTLE SHIRT THAT MOTHER MADE (FOR ME) "Learned from boys at WLS." The "boys at WLS" were the same ones from which he learned "Ain't We Crazy."

THE INNOCENT PRISONER "I wrote words and music."

IT MAKES NO DIFFERENCE NOW "You know all about that–Jimmy Davis. I met him in Southern Music Publishing Company's office one time years ago. He is on the list of those who will be at the Hall of Fame which I am on my way to attend now. His wife is also on list." (by Floyd Tillman, 1939)

JIMMIE RODGERS' LIFE "Bob Miller wrote words, and I wrote the tune."

JOHNNY SANDS "I would say this is an English-type folk song, comedy, that is." (Brown II, 488ff)

JUST AS THE SUN WENT DOWN "An old Civil War song." (Karl Kennett, wds., Lyn Udall, mus., 1898)

JUST PLAIN FOLKS "Can't remember where I got that." (by Maurice Stonehill, 1901)

THE KICKING MULE "I learned from my father."

THE KINGDOM COMING "From my father." (by Henry C. Work, 1862)

THE LAST ROUNDUP "Published song of the 30's. Very popular for a short period." (by Billy Hill)

THE LEGEND OF THE ROBIN'S RED BREAST "That was one of the last numbers I wrote. I made that for Capitol [Records]." The words were written by Blanche Preston Jones of Ashland, Kentucky. Brad paid her $25.00 for them and composed the tune. (The legend has been reported from Ireland and the United States–from Ireland in the IFC Mss., and Pete Welding heard it from his parents in Chicago.) (DKW)

LET THAT MULE GO AUNK Another title for "Kicking Mule." (DKW)
LETTER EDGED IN BLACK "A published song. I think I first heard Jack and Gene sing it." (by Hattie Nevada, 1897)
LIFE'S RAILWAY TO HEAVEN "I found it in songbooks. I first heard it from Asher and Little Jimmie. Asher was the one I heard sing that first." (M.E. Abbey, wds., Chas. D. Tillman, mus., 1890)
THE LIGHTNING EXPRESS (Don't Put Me Off the Train) "I think it was a published song . . . before the Gay Nineties." Apparently Brad still has a copyright on this. He recalls receiving payments a few years ago. (DKW) ("Please Mr. Conductor," by J. Fred Helf and E.P. Moran, 1898)
THE LILY OF THE WEST "Old traditional song." (Laws P 29)
LISTEN TO THE MOCKING BIRD "An old fiddle tune. I gathered a lot of the words to it and used to sing it. It is used as a sort of candystick for a great many old-time fiddlers who want something soft and sweet to show their style, not something real fast." (Septimus Winner, wds., Richard Milburn (?), mus., 1855)
LITTLE BLACK MOUSTACHE "I believe I learned that from Lulu Belle." (Randolph III, 128; by John Foster and R.A. King, 1926)
LITTLE BROWN JUG "Sung by quite a few people at WLS when I first went there. Chubby Parker used to sing it." (by J.E. Winner, 1869)
LITTLE DARLIN' DON'T SAY WE ARE THROUGH "I'm not too proud of it—but I wrote it in the fifties and recorded for Capitol. It never clicked."
LITTLE GREEN VALLEY "I used to hear Grandpa Jones sing that and Carson Robison used to sing it. I don't know, he might have written it."
LITTLE JOE "Old traditional song." (cf. Randolph IV, 173)
LITTLE JOE, THE WRANGLER "Somebody sent to me." (N. Howard "Jack" Thorp, wds., 1898; Laws B 5)
LITTLE MAN YOU'VE HAD A BUSY DAY "A popular song, published by Feist in the forties. I sang it only occasionally."
THE LITTLE MOHEE "An Indian song I would say is traditional." He told me he learned it from his family. (DKW) (Laws H 8)
LITTLE OLD LOG CABIN IN THE LANE "Of course everybody knows that. Came out of minstrel tradition. Same tune as 'The Lily of the Valley.' I think 'The Lily of the Valley' came later. A plantation song." (by Will S. Hays, 1871)
LITTLE RED ROOSTER AND THE OLD BLACK HEN "This was a poem sent to me by a fan. I put a tune to it and used it on radio. It was never much of a sensation."
LITTLE ROSEWOOD CASKET A "very old" song in Brad's home community. (DKW) ("A Package of Old Love Letters," by Louis P. Goullaud

& C.A. White, 1870)
THE LITTLE WHITEWASHED CHIMNEY "I learned from Doc Hopkins." (by Tex Fletcher, 19- -)
LIZA UP A 'SIMMON TREE "Learned from my father. When I wasn't more than four years old my father had me singing that for company and they'd just laugh."
LONG, LONG AGO "Same as 'Happy Days Long Ago.' "
LOOK ME IN THE EYE, JOHNNIE "Found in collection."
THE LOVE OF ROSANNA MCCOY "A poem sent to me by a lady up the Big Sandy. I put a tune to it but never used it."
MAMMY'S PRECIOUS BABY "I wrote in collaboration with one of the boys who used to sing in the quartet on WLS."
THE MAN ON THE FLYING TRAPEZE "A popular song of the eighties, made popular again by Rudy Vallee in the forties. I used it some." (composer unknown, 1868)
MANSION OF ACHING HEARTS "In same category as 'After the Ball,' 'Two Little Girls in Blue,' and a lot of these others we've just gone through here." (Arthur Lamb, wds., Harry Von Tilzer, mus., 1902)
MARTINS AND THE COYS "Made popular by a southern band leader."
MARY WORE THREE LINKS OF CHAIN "Had its origin among the Negroes of the South. An old spiritual. Used it a long time. Don't remember where I learned it." He identified this as a family song. (DKW) (Brown III, 600)
METHODIST PIE "A comedy song. Man wrote it after going to Camp Nelson, Kentucky, to hear circuit rider preachers at old-fashioned Methodist camp meetings. I don't think it was ever published until maybe when I published it in one of my books." (Randolph II, 375) (="An Old Camp Meeting")
THE MINER'S SONG "This fellow that was doing the recording session [for Majestic] brought down the sheet music and asked me to learn it." Mr. Gilmore of Southern Music sent Brad a test recording from the author and Brad then recorded it at a Majestic session. (DKW)
THE MISTLETOE BOUGH "An old traditional song." (by Thomas H. Bayly, 18- -)
MOLLY DARLING "I first heard Eddy Arnold sing that when I was down at the Opry. Could almost be called a traditional song, but I think it was published." (by Will S. Hays, 1871)
MOLLY MALONE (Recorded for Bluebonnet)
THE MORE WE GET TOGETHER "Where did you get that? Was that in my collection? It's an old round thing. I've sung it many times, but not on the air."

MY GRANDFATHER'S CLOCK "Everybody knows all about 'My Grandfather's Clock.' I don't think I can add anything. A published song." (by Henry C. Work, 1876)
MY JEAN "A classical song I used to sing before I got into radio and started to sing mountain ballads." (by Caro Roma)
MY LITTLE HOME IN TENNESSEE "I think I got that from Hugh Cross." (by Carson Robison, 19 ?)
MY MOTHER'S (BEAUTIFUL) HANDS "An old traditional song. I learned from Shortbuckle Roark up here at Manchester, Ky., on a song hunting tour with Dave Thompson from WLS. We came through Berea and I did a program at Chapel here that was the best audience I ever had. In about 1927 or 1928." (Originally "My Mother's Hands," by Mrs. M.E. Wilson, ?)
MY MOTHER'S OLD RED SHAWL "I don't know where I learned that, but it was old and popular with my radio audience over the years." (by Chas. Mouland (Moreland?), 1886)
MY PRETTY QUADROON (by Mary Dodge, 1863; revised by Nat Vincent, 1930)
MY SWEET IOLA "A published song my mother and father used to sing." (O'Dea & Johnson, 1906)
NICKITTY NACKITTY NOW NOW NOW "Learned from Chubby Parker at WLS when I first went there." (Randolph III, 191)
NO COMPROMISE "Mine, but I'm not proud of it."
NO, I WON'T HAVE HIM (The Old Man Who Came Over the Moor) "One my father sang." (Brown III, 17)
NO JOHN NO "That is an old English ballad. It's in almost any collection you'll find. I think I just picked it out of one of those old English songbooks." (Sharp IV, (1908), 46)
NO SIR NO "An old timer. Two versions of that—both English type songs. Other is 'No John No.' " (Randolph III, 104)
NOBODY'S DARLING "A published song about 1930-1937 somewhere in there." (by Jimmie Davis, 1935)
NOW I LAY ME DOWN TO SLEEP "Ford Rush used to sing this as a theme song." (Sidney D. Mitchell, wds., Geo. W. Meyer, mus., 1920)
NOW THE TABLE'S TURNED ON YOU "I wrote and recorded that for Capitol."
OL' COON DOG "Old fiddle tune."
THE OLD ACCOUNT WAS SETTLED (LONG AGO) "An old hymn I've known for many years."
OLD DAN TUCKER "Old fiddle tune." (by Dan Emmett, 1843)
OLD JOE CLARK "Old fiddle tune. Old Joe Clark lived up in Manchester,

Kentucky. In my collecting of songs I visited Manchester, Ky., and heard from the man who ran the hotel there and several of the citizens the same story about Old Joe Clark." Brad added that Old Joe Clark was killed by his son. Clark was a notorious character. He carried a long knife down the back of his neck all the time so that he could reach it and get it quickly. The Betty Brown that is mentioned in the song was living with Joe by force. One day Joe's hogs got out and got into the corn field of his son on the adjoining farm. The son got his shotgun and killed Old Joe, which was the very thing that the girl (Betty Brown) wanted so she could get away from him. (DKW) (Sharp II, 259)

THE OLD KITCHEN FLOOR "Another traditional song."

OLD NUMBER THREE "Is a real folk song. Words written by a preacher–the story of an engineer–a train wreck. Often called 'Billy Richardson's Last Ride.' Learned from a record made by Carson Robison and Vernon Dalhart." (Originally "Billy Richardson's Last Ride," C.C. Meeks, wds., Carson Robison, mus., 1926)

OLD SHEP (by Red Foley)

OLD SMOKY "What I do is a combination of 'Waggoner Lad' and 'Old Smoky.' " Learned from family. (DKW) (Sharp II, 123)

THE OLD WOODEN ROCKER "Old traditional song." (by Florence Harper, 1878)

ONLY A FACE FRAMED IN GOLD "Another unsuccessful one of mine."

THE ORPHAN GIRL "Was handed down by word of mouth." (Brown II, 388 ff.)

ONLY AS FAR AS THE GATE "A cute little song I found in a collection and learned."

PEACH PICKING TIME DOWN IN GEORGIA "A song that was published; by Clayton McMichen." (by Jimmie Rodgers & Clayton McMichen, 1933)

PADDLE YOUR OWN CANOE "Was a copyrighted song. When I first went to WLS in Chicago the treasurer of the *Prairie Farmer* who bought WLS from Sears Roebuck brought me the sheet-music and asked me to learn it and sing it because he liked it so well. And I did. The *Prairie Farmer* was a farm paper." (by Harry Clifton?, 1870s)

PAPER OF PINS "Handed down by word of mouth." (Randolph III, 40)

PEARL BRYAN "Don't know who wrote it." Brad was familiar with the tune in Kentucky and connected it with "The Jealous Lover." He could not recall the source of the words. (DKW) (Laws F 16)

PEEPIN' THROUGH THE KEYHOLE OF GRANDPA'S WOODEN LEG "Reasonably funny."

PERI MERI DINCTUM "Handed down by word of mouth."

THE PICTURE OF LIFE'S OTHER SIDE "Old 'tear jerker.' Very popular with me on radio." (by Chas. E. Baer, 1896)
A PRETTY FAIR MAID "Handed down by word of mouth." (Laws N 42)
PRETTY LITTLE BIRD "Same as 'Free A Little Bird As I Can Be.' Learned from Doc Hopkins."
PRETTY LITTLE DEVILISH MARY "Handed down by word of mouth." (Laws Q 4)
PRETTY LITTLE PINK "Another one I got from Skyland Scotty [Wiseman]." (Brown III, 110)
PRETTY POLLY "Sometimes called 'The House Carpenter.' " Old traditional song. Probably means "The Ship's Carpenter." (DKW) (Laws P 366)
PUT MY LITTLE SHOES AWAY "Learned from Jack and Jerry Foy." (by Chas. E. Pratt & Samuel N. Mitchell, 1873)
RABBITS IN THE LOWLANDS "An old fiddle tune."
RATTLER "Song about a dog. I learned that from Grandpa Jones."
THE RED RIVER VALLEY "Everybody knows that. I suppose I heard it as a kid but I remember it was used quite frequently by people who came to WLS in the early days of radio." (Originally "In the Bright Mohawk Valley," by James J. Kerrigan, 1896)
RED WING
REUBEN, WHERE'VE YOU BEEN SO LONG? "Old-traditional, in the same category and reminescent of the period of 'John Henry.' "
RIDIN' DOWN THAT OLD KENTUCKY TRAIL
RIP VAN WINKLE (Rip Van Winkle Was a Lucky Man, by Jerome & Schwartz, 1901)
ROCKING ALONE (In An Old Rocking Chair) "I learned that from Grandpa Jones about forty years ago."
ROLL ALONG KENTUCKY MOON "I learned from Grandpa Jones." (by Bill Halley, 1932)
THE ROVING KIND "I am not sure of the origin. Arthur Godfrey sang it when he was on radio. I think it was a revised old English folk song."
SAN ANTONIO "A cowboy song I have known since my youth." (by Harry H. Williams and Egbert Van Alstyne, 1907)
SAN ANTONIO ROSE (by Bob Wills; first entitled "Spanish Two-Step," rearranged by S.A. Rose in the 1930s and recorded under that title in 1938; words added later, titled "New San Antonio Rose.")
SCHOOL DAYS (by Will D. Cobb and Gus Edwards, 1907)
SHE WAS BRED IN OLD KENTUCKY "Another one I learned from my father. A published song." (by Harry Braisted & Stanley Carter, 1898)
SHE'LL BE COMIN' 'ROUND THE MOUNTAIN "There's no use saying anything about "She'll Be Comin' 'Round the Mountain.' " (Brown III,

534)

SHE'S NOT A BIT WORSE FOR THAT "This must have been a published song of the late nineties. I heard my father sing it, and years later, others."

SHE WAS HAPPY TILL SHE MET YOU "A published song of 1900's, like 'After the Ball,' 'Two Little Girls in Blue,' etc." (by Charles Graham and Monroe Rosenfeld)

THE SHIP THAT NEVER RETURNED "Is in the old category. Old English type song." (by Henry C. Work, 1865; Laws D 27)

SILVER HAIRED DADDY OF MINE "Remember Gene Autry?" (by Dan Kane, 1931)

SLEEP, BABY, SLEEP "Almost a classic in the yodeling field." (by John J. Handley, 1885)

SLEEPY-HEAD "I wrote."

SOLDIER, SOLDIER, WILL YOU MARRY ME? "Old English type song." (Randolph I, 289)

SOME LITTLE BUG IS GOING TO FIND YOU "I wrote the melody to that. Somebody sent me the words."

SOMEBODY'S WAITING FOR YOU "A published song." (by Albert Gumble and Vincent Bryan, 19--)

SONG THE COW DIED ON (From mid-1800s or earlier. See Randolph, OFS, III, 148)

SOURWOOD MOUNTAIN "That goes along with all these early ones like 'Liza Up in the 'Simmon Tree.' An old fiddle tune. My father used to sing the words to it. Always known." Worked up his version from a number of sources. The order and arrangement are his. He said that in such songs he sometimes had to make up verses to fill gaps or to fill out a phonograph record, and also at times had to revise apparent obscenities. (DKW) (Sharp II, 305)

STEAMBOAT BILL "A published song." (by Ren Shields & Leighton Bros., 1910)

STRAWBERRY ROAN "A published song." (by Fred Howard and Curly Fletcher, 1941)

THE STREETS OF LAREDO "A traditional cowboy number. I can't remember these fellows' names now. It was back in 1928-29 there was a stream of cowboys and folk singers and people like Gid Tanner that would come from the west. They would hear about how popular WLS Radio was and they would come. I remember some cowboy came by and I learned 'When the Work's All Done This Fall.' " Brad knew the "Dying Cowboy" version from his Kentucky boyhood. He later heard the "Streets of Laredo" tune while at WLS in Chicago and set his words to the tune (Gennett). (DKW) (Laws B 1)

STUTTERING SONG "I learned that from a girl who worked with me on a tent show many years ago."

SUNSHINE OF PARADISE ALLEY (by Walter H. Ford and John W. Bratton, 1895)

THE SWAPPING SONG Learned from his family. (DKW)

SWEET BETSY FROM PIKE "Learned from Doc Hopkins." (Laws B 9)

SWEET INNISCARRA* He didn't remember it at first, but later recalled that it was from the Kapp-Decca session, as "Tumble Down Shack in Athlone." (DKW) (Sang with his wife playing the piano.) (Augustus Pitou, wds., Chauncey Olcott, mus., 1897)

SWEET KITTY WELLS "Another one I would say is practically traditional, although it could have been published back in the 80s." From his father. (DKW) (by Thomas Sloane, 1860s)

SWING LOW, SWEET CHARIOT "Another Negro type."

SWING THE LADIES UP AND DOWN "It used to be very much against the principles of the church officials for the young people to dance. So the young people worked up these games and they would sing the tune."

THE GREAT WHITE BIRD "A legend. Words sent to me by Blanche Preston Jones, Ashland, Kentucky. I composed the tune."

THAT OLD TINTYPE PICTURE " I wrote."

THAT TUMBLE DOWN SHACK IN ATHLONE* "Jack Kapp who organized Decca Records had me do half a dozen songs with my wife playing the piano." (Richard W. Pascoe, wds., Monte Carlo & Alma Sanders, mus., 1918)

THERE NEVER WAS A PAL LIKE MOTHER "Learned from Doc Hopkins."

THERE'S A MOTHER OLD AND GRAY WHO NEEDS YOU "Another published song of the nineties."

THERE WAS AN OLD SOLDIER "An old one."

THERE'S A LOVE KNOT IN MY LARIAT "Wilf Carter, who wrote this, and I became friends in the late thirties, and he asked me to use this song on my programs, which I did occasionally.

THERE'S NO PLACE LIKE HOME "Now what you are probably referring to here is a comedy song that I used. I used to use it on the stage and I had it in my books."

THERE'S A RED LIGHT AHEAD "I wrote myself when I was at Nashville." Written on a personal appearance, stimulated by an actual happening. (DKW)

THEY CUT DOWN THE OLD PINE TREE "A published song of the forties—maybe thirties—and quite popular for a while. I used it frequently. It was often requested."

THOSE PRECIOUS LOVE LETTERS "I can't think of the fellow's name who wrote that, but I recorded it at Majestic."
THREE WISHES "Learned from my father." ("Better Than Gold, or Three Wishes," by Chas. K. Harris, 1895)
TILDY JOHNSON "Learned from my father."
TRAVEL ON, LITTLE PONY "A cowboy song of the thirties. I learned it from Grandpa Jones."
TREASURE UNTOLD "Grandpa Jones used to sing this." (by Jimmie Rodgers & Ellsworth T. Cozzens, 1928)
THE TRUE AND TREMBLING BRAKEMAN "I learned from an uncle of mine–Ben Kincaid." (Laws G 11)
THE TRUE LOVER'S FAREWELL "Old English type song." (Sharp II, 113)
THE TURKISH LADY "My mother used to sing this." (="Lord Bateman," Child No. 53)
TWENTY YEARS AGO "Found in old collection." (Dill Armor Smith, wds., Wm. Willing, mus., ca. 1846)
TWO LITTLE FROGS "A song that dates back to the days of Good Queen Bess. Same as 'Froggie Went A-Courtin'.' (The tune, refrain and chorus are similar to those sometimes used in 'Froggie Went A-Courtin' but the story is not the same.)
TWO LITTLE BLUE LITTLE SHOES "Very, very old and a touching story. Sent to me. I used it some on radio. Not too popular.
TWO LITTLE GIRLS IN BLUE "One of my father's favorites. A publishing company in Philadelphia had originally published it and while it should have been in the public domain by then, they had recopyrighted it. This fellow found one of my old songbooks and he wrote to me and said he thought it would be in very good taste if I sent him a check for fifty dollars, which I reluctantly did." (by Chas. Graham, 1893)
TWO SISTERS "A very old English ballad." From his family. (DKW) (Child No. 10)
TYING THE LEAVES From Grandpa Jones. (DKW)
UTAH CARROLL "Somebody sent to me." (Laws B 4)
VILLAGE BY THE SEA (cf. Randolph WFS IV, 321; probably late 19th C.)
WABASH CANNON BALL "A song of great fame. I'm still waiting for somebody to give me an explanation of what that means." (parody on "The Great Rock Island Route," by J.A. Roff, 1882)
WAIT, MR. POSTMAN "An old published song of the eighties."
THE WAGONER LAD "Traditional. Notice the text to 'Old Smoky.' I combined the two to make a song long enough to record–three minutes

at that time. (Brown III, 275 ff.)

WAIT FOR THE WAGON PHILLIS "A published song."

THE WAYFARING PILGRIM "An old hymn used by Burl Ives as his theme song in the early forties.

WHAT'LL I DO WITH THE BABY-O? "Seems like I've always known it." (Sharp II, 336)

WHAT ARE WE MADE OF "I call it 'What's a Little Boy Made Of.' Learned from parents."

WHEN I FIT WITH GENERAL GRANT Learned from Foster Brooks, an announcer on a Louisville radio station. (DKW)

WHEN IRISH EYES ARE SMILING* "A published song." This is also from the Kapp-Decca session. (DKW) (by Ernest Ball, 1910)

WHEN IT'S NIGHT-TIME IN NEVADA "I got from Grandpa Jones." (by H. O'Reilly Clint & Will E. Dulmage, 19- -)

WHEN IT'S TIME FOR THE WHIPPOORWILLS TO SING (Recorded by Delmore Bros., 1940; probably written by Alton Delmore)

WHEN JESUS BECKONS ME HOME "I got from Grandpa Jones."

WHEN MY BLUE MOON TURNS TO GOLD AGAIN "It was published in the forties, and for a short time was mildly popular. I used it a few times." (by Wiley Walker and Gene Sullivan, 1941)

WHEN THE ROSES BLOOM AGAIN (by Will D. Cobb and Gus Edwards, 1901)

WHEN THE STATION CLOCK STRUCK FOUR (by Bradley Kincaid and Clarence Stout)

WHEN THE WHIPPOORWILL SINGS, MARGUERITE "A published song of the early nineties. I can recall hearing my sister singing this, using the original 'Houn' Dog' guitar." (by C.M. Denison and J. Fred Helf)

WHEN THE WORK'S ALL DONE THIS FALL "Learned from a cowboy." Learned from "Peg" Moreland (then known as "Tex") when Moreland was performing on WLS. (DKW) (D.J. O'Malley, wds., 1893; Laws B 3)

WHERE IS MY WANDERING BOY TONIGHT "One of heart breakers of many years ago." (by Robert Lowery, 1937)

WHERE THE SILV'RY COLORADO WENDS ITS WAY (by C.H. Scroggins and Charles Avril, 1901)

WHERE WERE YOU LAST SATURDAY NIGHT "Traditional, and sounds English." (Brown III, 299 ff.)

WHISPERING HOPE "Very traditional. Published at one time many years ago." (by Septimus Winner, 1868)

WILD BILL JONES "Ranks with John Henry in time. In substance it is characteristic of many of the hill or mountain variety of rowdy, jealousy-inspired songs."

WILL THE ANGELS PLAY THEIR HARPS FOR ME "I can't remember the fellow's name who wrote it, but it was about the time I went to WLS. I had been there about a year I guess and I was doing my first recording session and this fellow had just written this song and he asked me to record it, and I did." (by Hirsch & Wilhite, 19- -)

WILLIE DOWN BY THE POND "Another old traditional one." (Laws G 19)

WILLIS MAYBERRY (=Hills of Roane County)

WON'T YOU COME OVER TO MY HOUSE "A published song I learned from my father going back to the eighties. Popular with my radio fans." (by Harry H. Williams and Egbert Van Alystyne, 1907)

WORK, FOR THE NIGHT IS COMING "An old traditional hymn." (Annie W. Coghill, wds., 1854; Lowell Mason, mus., 1865)

THE WRECK OF THE NUMBER NINE "I heard Pie Plant Pete sing that." (by Carson Robison, 1927; Laws G 26)

THE WRECK ON THE C. & O. ROAD "I can tell you something rather funny about that. After I had sung this one time on WLW—about the first time I sang it there—when I left WLS and came to WLW—I did that number on an afternoon program and pretty soon after, the president of the C. & O. Road called the management of WLW and said, 'That song that man sang just cost us about a hundred thousand dollars.' Now can you imagine that. I quit singing it." Brad indicated to me that his source was Cox. (DKW) (Laws G 3)

THE YELLOW ROSE OF TEXAS (late 1850s; author not identified)

YOU ARE MY SUNSHINE "Jimmy Davis." (by Jas. H. Davis & Chas. Mitchell, 1940)

YOU CAN'T EAT YOUR CAKE AND STILL HAVE IT "Another of my efforts."

YOU GO TO YOUR CHURCH AND I'LL GO TO MINE "A hymn popular in the thirties. I used it occasionally in radio.

YOUNG CHARLOTTE "Sometimes called 'Frozen Girl.' Supposed to be a true story. Happened up in Vermont. A young man took her to a dance and before she got there, she froze to death." (Originally "A Corpse Going To a Ball," by Seba Smith, 1843; Laws G 17)

YOUNG ROGERS THE MILLER "Old English ballad." (Laws P 8)

ZEBRA DUN "Another one of those songs that was sent in to me." (Laws B 16)

ZEB TOURNEY'S GAL "I don't know it too well because I learned it and published it in, I think, my Number 4 songbook, and I had a nice letter from Carson Robison informing me that the song had been written by a women he knew. I told him I wouldn't use it in further publication." (by Marjorie Lamkin & Maggie Andrews = Carson Robison, 1926; Laws E 18)

Addendum: The following hymns appeared on *Bradley Kincaid, Family Gospel Album* (McMonigle, BK3, BK4) which was released after the checklist was completed.
AMAZING GRACE "I've sung that all my life." (by John Newton)
I AM NOT ASHAMED OF JESUS "That is a song that was written by Leo McMonigle who put out the hymn album."
NINETY AND NINE "Learned forty years ago." (by Elizabeth C. Clephane and Ira D. Sankey)
THE OLD RUGGED CROSS "Known it all my life." (by Rev. George Bennard)
SHOWERS OF BLESSING "Learned years ago." (by Daniel W. Whittle)
SINCE THE CROSS CAST ITS SHADOW ON ME "Another one of Leo McMonigle's songs."
THERE'S A CHURCH IN THE VALLEY (The Church in the Wildwood) "Learned way back." (by William Pitts)
THE UNCLOUDED DAY "I learned that years ago." (by J.K. Alwood)

*The Kapp-Decca session seems to have involved Kapp bringing him material which Brad and his wife performed—for the United States and overseas Irish market. (DKW)

APPENDIX B
Published Songbooks*

No. 1 *Favorite Mountain Ballads and Old Time Songs* (Later editions, *My Favorite Mountain Ballads and Old-Time Songs*), Chicago, WLS,
First Printing, April, 1928
Second Printing, May, 1928
Third Printing, November, 1928
Fourth Printing, January, 1929
Fifth Printing, February, 1929
Sixth Printing, July, 1929

No. 2 *Favorite Old-Time Songs and Mountain Ballads*, Chicago, WLS, 1929.

No. 3 *Favorite Old-Time Songs and Mountain Ballads*, Chicago, WLS, 1930.

No. 4 *My Favorite Old Time Songs and Mountain Ballads*, Cincinnati, WLW, 1931.

No. 5 *My Favorite Mountain Ballads and Old Time Songs*, Pittsburgh, KDKA, 1932.

No. 6 *Mountain Ballads and Old Time Songs*, Location not indicated. Probably WGY, Schenectady or WEAF, New York. No date. 1933 or 1934.

No. 7 *Mountain Ballads, Old Time Songs*, Boston, WBZ, 1936.

No. 8 *Favorite Mountain Ballads and Old Time Songs*, New York: Southern Music Publishing Co. Inc., 1937 (20 songs).

No. 9 *Mountain Ballads*, Garden City, New York, 1939.

There was no No. 10. Bradley viewed the deluxe edition of No. 8 brought out by Southern Music Co. as No. 10.

No. 11 *Mountain Ballads, Old Time Songs*, Rochester, WHAM, 1940.

No. 12 *Bradley Kincaid Folio No. 12*, New York: Peer International Corp., 1941.

No. 13 *Mountain Ballads and Old Time Songs*, Nashville, WSM. No date. Probably 1945 or 1946.

Note: Three songbooks changed covers between printings or editions. No. 1, No. 7 and No. 9 have two different covers with the contents unchanged. No. 8 has minor cover changes in three editions, with the songs expanded from 20 to 50 from the first to the second edition. See the following photographs and pp. 53-54.

*The writer appreciates help from Archie Green and Nicholas Vangoff in straightening out the puzzle of the songbooks.

W L S THE SEARS, ROEBUCK RADIO STATION
Favorite Mountain Ballads
and
Old Time Songs
as sung by
Bradley Kincaid
"The Mountain Boy"
CHICAGO . . . . . ILLINOIS

My Favorite
Mountain Ballads
—and—
Old-Time Songs..
Bradley Kincaid
As Sung Over
WLS
The
PRAIRIE FARMER
STATION

"THE MOUNTAIN BOY"
Favorite
Old-Time Songs
and Mountain Ballads
Book 2

FAVORITE OLD-TIME SONGS
and MOUNTAIN BALLADS
Book 3

My Favorite
Old Time Songs
and
Mountain Ballads
WLW
Bradley Kincaid

MY FAVORITE Mountain Ballads
and OLD TIME SONGS
Bradley Kincaid

MOUNTAIN BALLADS
and
OLD TIME SONGS
Bradley Kincaid
"THE KENTUCKY MOUNTAIN BOY"
Book 6
Price 50 cents

MOUNTAIN BALLADS
Old Time Songs.
BRADLEY KINCAID
BOOK #7
PRICE 50¢

MOUNTAIN BALLADS
Old Time Songs.
BRADLEY KINCAID
BOOK #7
PRICE 50¢

BRADLEY KINCAID
THE KENTUCKY MOUNTAIN BOY
Favorite
MOUNTAIN
BALLADS
AND
OLD TIME SONGS
NO. 8
Including
"THE LITTLE SHIRT THAT MOTHER MADE FOR ME"
"WHISPERING HOPE"
"PADDLE YOUR OWN CANOE"
"I LOVE MY ROOSTER"
as sung by
BRADLEY KINCAID
SOUTHERN MUSIC PUB. CO., INC.

BRADLEY KINCAID
THE KENTUCKY MOUNTAIN BOY
Favorite
MOUNTAIN
BALLADS
AND
OLD TIME SONGS
50 SONGS
WITH GUITAR, TENOR BANJO AND UKULELE CHORDS
Including
"THE LITTLE SHIRT THAT MOTHER MADE FOR ME"
"WHISPERING HOPE"
"PADDLE YOUR OWN CANOE"
"I LOVE MY ROOSTER"
as sung by
BRADLEY KINCAID
SOUTHERN MUSIC PUB. CO., INC.

DE LUXE EDITION
BRADLEY KINCAID
THE KENTUCKY MOUNTAIN BOY
Favorite
MOUNTAIN
BALLADS
AND
OLD TIME SONGS
50
as sung by
BRADLEY KINCAID

Songbook photos by Nicholas Vangoff

APPENDIX C
DISCOGRAPHY

This discography was prepared by Norm Cohen of the John Edwards Memorial Foundation to accompany an article on Bradley Kincaid in the *JEMF Quarterly* (Autumn 1976) and is used by permission.

All sides are by Bradley Kincaid, vocal and guitar, unless noted otherwise. Record label abbreviations as follows: Gen = Gennett, Chm = Champion, Chl = Challange, Sil = Silvertone, Spt = Supertone, Bel = Bell, Spr = Superior, MW = Montgomery Ward, Br = Brunswick, Cq = Conqueror, Vo = Vocalion, DeI = Irish Decca, Me = Melotone, MeC = Melotone (Canada), RZAu = Australian Regal Zonophone, Po = Polk, Pan = English Panachord (with P prefix, Australian), Bb = Bluebird, El = Electradisk, Su = Sunrise.

Names of companies, dates and identifying numbers listed to the left of the page indicate the recording sessions and the material that was recorded. The listing of label numbers to the right of the page is the material as it was released on record labels. Often the same numbers were released on two or more labels.

Starr Piano Co., ca. 19 Dec. 1927, Chicago, Ill.

GE-13312 The Fatal Wedding
Gen 6363, Chm 15248, Chl 366, Sil 5186, Sil 8217, Spt 9211, Bel 1178

GE-13313A Sweet Kitty Wells
Gen 6363

Note: After 22 Oct. 1929, mx GE-13313 was replaced by GE-15746.
All Champions issued as by Dan Hughey; Bell 1178 as by John Carpenter

Starr Piano Co., ca. 27 Feb. 1928, Chicago, Ill.

GE-13472 Barbara Allen
Spt 9211 Sil 5186, Sil 8217

GE-13473 Methodist Pie
Gen 6417, Chm 15631, Sil 5189, Sil 8220
Spt 9210

GE-13474 Froggie Went A-Courtin'
Gen 6462, Chm 15466, Sil 5188, Sil 8219
Spt 9209

Note: Chm 15631 was titled "An Old Camp Meeting" instead of "Methodist Pie."

Starr Piano Co., ca. 28 Feb. 1928, Chicago, Ill.

GE-13478A Sourwood Mountain
Gen 6417, Chm 15466, Chl 366, Sil 5189, Sil 8220
Spt 9210, Bel 1178

GE-13479 The Swapping Song
Gen 6462, Chm 15466, Sil 5188, Sil 8219
Spt 9209

GE-13480A Bury Me on the Prairie
Sil 5187, Sil 8218
Spt 9208, Spr 2588

Note: Spr 2588 issued as by Harley Stratton; A take used.

Starr Piano Co., ca. 9 Mar. 1928, Chicago, Ill.

GE-13520 Paper of Pins
Rejected

GE-13521 The Turkish Lady
Rejected

GE-13522 The Two Sisters (The Miller)
Rejected

GE-13523 Fair Ellen
Rejected

Starr Piano Co., ca. 9 Mar. 1928, Chicago, Ill.

WLS Showboat sides are by several artists, including Kincaid.

GE-13549 The (WLS) Showboat—Part I
Sil 5199, Sil 8231

GE-13552 The (WLS) Showboat—Part II
Sil 5199, Sil 8231

Starr Piano Co., ca. 9 Mar. 1928, Chicago, Ill.

GE-13575 The Little Rosewood Casket
Rejected

GE-13576 The (WLS) Showboat–Part III
Sil 5200, Sil 8232

GE-13577 The (WLS) Showboat–Part IV
Sil 5200, Sil 8232

GE-13578A The Ship That Never Returned
Rejected

GE-13581A Barney McCoy
Rejected

GE-13582A Don't Put Me Off the Train
Rejected

GE-13587 The (WLS) Showboat–Part V
Sil 5201, Sil 8233

GE-13588 The (WLS) Showboat–Part VI
Sil 5201, Sil 8233

Note regarding takes: All Starr recordings utilized three takes–"plain," A, and B. Only the issued take(s) is shown in this discography.

Starr Piano Co., ca. 12 July 1928, Chicago, Ill.

GE-14028 Pearl Bryan
Rejected

GE-14029 Rip Van Winkle
Rejected

GE-14030 Liza Up in the Sim'mon Tree
Rejected

GE-14031A Cuckoo Is a Pretty Bird
Gen 6620

GE-14032 Four Thousand Years Ago
Rejected

GE-14033 Don't Put Me Off the Train
Rejected

GE-14034 Soldier, Soldier, Will You Marry Me
Rejected

GE-14035 Little Mohee
Rejected

GE-14036 Butcher Boy
Rejected

GE-14037 I Loved You Better than You Knew
Rejected

GE-14038 Billy Boy
Rejected

GE-14039 Fair Ellen
Spt 9212 Sil 8221

GE-14040 Two Sisters
Spt 9212 Sil 8221

GE-14041 Paper of Pins
Rejected

GE-14042 Red River Valley
Rejected

GE-14043 The Orphan Girl
Rejected

Starr Piano Co., 28 Jan. 1929, Richmond, Ind.

GE-14738 Four Thousand Years Ago
Gen 6761, Chm 15687, Chm 45057, Spt 9362,
Spr 2656

GE-14739 When the Work's All Done This Fall
Gen 6989

GE-14740 Give My Love to Nell
Gen 7020 Spt 9350

GE-14741B In the Streets of Laredo
Gen 6790 Spt 9404

GE-14742AB The Wreck On the C. & O. Road
Gen 6823, Chm 15710, Chm 45098, Spt 9350
MeC 45057

GE-14743 Pearl Bryan
Gen 6823, Chm 15731, Spt 9404

GE-14744B The Little Mohee
Gen 6856, Chm 15731, Spt 9402

GE-14745 The Red River Valley
Gen 6790, Chm 15710, Chm 45098, Spt 9403,
Spr 2588

GE-14746A Liza Up In the 'Simmon Tree
Gen 6761, Chm 15687, Chm 45057, Spt 9362,
MeC 45067

GE-14747 The Little Rosewood Casket
Gen 6989, Spt 9403

GE-14748 A Paper of Pins
Gen 6856, Spt 9402

Notes: GE-14742: A take used on Gen, B take on Chm; GE-14746: "plain" take used on Gen, A take on Chm and MeC. Spr 2588 issued as by Harley Stratton.

Starr Piano Co., ca 7 June 1929, Richmond, Ind.

GE-15163A Happy Days Long Ago
Gen 6944, Chm 15787, Spt 9471

GE-15168 Little Old Log Cabin in the Lane
Gen 6958, Chm 15923, Spt 9505

GE-15169 Will the Angels Play Their Harps for Me
Gen 6900, Chm 15771, Chm 45130, Spt 9452

GE-15170 Charlie Brooks
Gen 6958, Chm 16029, Chm 45039, Spt 9648, Spr 2788

GE-17171 Angels in Heaven Know I Love You
Gen 6900, Chm 15771, Chm 45130, Spt 9452

GE-17172 Let That Mule Go Aunk! Aunk!
Gen 6944, Chm 15787, Spt 9471, Spr 2656

GE-17173 Old Number Three
Gen 7020, Chm 15923, Spt 9505, Spr 2788

GE-17174 Billy Boy
Rejected

Starr Piano Co., ca. 4 Oct. 1929, Richmond, Ind.

GE-15734A Cindy
Gen 7112, Chm 15851, Spt 9568, Spr 2770

GE-15735A My Little Home in Tennessee
Chm 15851, Spt 9568

GE-15736 On Top of Old Smoky
Gen 7053, Chm 16029, Chm 45039, Spt 9566, Spr 2770, MW M-4984

GE-15737 And So You Have Come Back to Me
Rejected

GE-15738A After the Ball
Gen 7081, Chm 15876, Spt 9648,
MeC 45002
GE-15739A I Will Be All Smiles Tonight
Gen 7053, Chm 15876, Spt 9566,
MeC 45002
GE-15740 Pretty Little Pink
Spt 9666
GE-15741A The Blind Girl
Gen 7081, Chm 15968, Spt 9565,
MW M-4984
GE-15742 De Ladies Man
Rejected
GE-15743A Mary Wore Three Links of Chain
Spt 9666
GE-15744 I Could Not Call Her Mother
Gen 7112, Chm 15968, Spt 9565
GE-15745 (Untitled)
Rejected
GE-15746B Sweet Kitty Wells
Gen 6363, Chm 15502, Sil 5187, Sil 8218,
Spt 9208

Note: On GE-15741—after 15 Apr. 1930 the A take was usec

Brunswick-Balke-Collender Co., 22 Nov. 1929, Chicago, Ill.

C-4732 Give My Love to Nell
Rejected; remade
C-4733 The Blind Girl
Rejected; remade
C-4734 Methodist Pie
Rejected; remade
C-4735 Sweet Kitty Wells
Rejected
C-4736 When the Work's All Done This Fall
Rejected; remade
C-4737 Barbara Allen
Rejected; remade
C-4738 Streets of Laredo
Rejected

Brunswick-Balke-Collender Co., ca. Feb. 1930, Chicago, Ill.

C-5302 When the Work's All Done this Fall
Br 403, Spt 2017
C-5303 Give My Love to Nell
Br 403, Spt 2017
C-5304 Methodist Pie
Br 420, Spt 2018
C-5305 Barbara Allen
Me 12349, Cq 7982, Vo 02685, DeI W4148
C-5306 The Blind Girl
Me 12349, Cq 7983, Vo 02685, DeI W4148
C-5307 Sourwood Mountain
Br 420, Spt 2018, Cq 8090

Brunswick-Balke-Collender Co., ca. mid-March 1930, Chicago, Ill.

C-5558 Cindy
Br 464, Br-80093 (in Album De-Br B-1025),
Br BL-59000, Coral (Japan) MH 174,
MCA (Japan) 3013
C-5559 Pretty Little Pink
Br 464

Note: BL-59000 was a 10 inch LP; De-Br B-1025 an album of 4 10 inch 78s, both titled *Mountain Frolic*, a reissue set compiled by Alan Lomax in ca. 1947.

Brunswick-Balke-Collender Co., ca. 8 Oct. 1930, Chicago, Ill.

C-6426 I Wish I Had Someone to Love Me
Me M12372, Vo 02686, RZAu G22216
C-6427 Old Joe Clark
Br 485, Cq 8090,
Br 80096 (in Album De-Br B-1025),
Br BL-59000
C-6428 Old Coon Dog
Br 485
C-6429 The Innocent Prisoner
Me M12372, Vo 02686, RZAu G22216

Brunswick-Balke-Collender Co., ca. mid-Dec. 1930, Chicago, Ill.

C-6865 Somewhere, Somebody's Waiting for You

C-6865 Cont.
Me M12262, Vo 02705, Cq 7984, Po 9079,
RZAu G22218

C-6866 The Fatal Derby Day
Me M12315, Vo 02684, RZAu G22215

C-6867 Red River Valley
Me M12183, Vo 5476, Vo 04647, ARC 7-06-71,
Po 9050, Pan P12183, DeI W4475

C-6868 A Picture From Life's Other Side
Me M12183, Vo 5476, Vo 04647, ARC 7-06-71,
Po 9050, Pan P12183, DeI W4475

C-6869 Two Little Girls in Blue
Me M12291, Vo 5475, Po 9093, Pan 25, DeI 4456
Sterling (Canada) 91316

C-6870 Gooseberry Pie
Me M12291, Vo 5475, Po 9093, Pan 25, DeI 4456
Sterling (Canada) 91316

C-6871 The Fatal Wedding
Me M12315, Vo 02684, Cq 7982, RZAu G22215

C-6872 Bury Me Out on the Prairie
Me M12332, Cq 8091, Vo 5474, ARC 7-06-70,
RZAu G22575

C-6873 The True and Trembling Brakeman
Me M12184, Cq 8091, Vo 02683, Po 9064, Pan 25,
Pan P12184

C-6874 The Lightning Express (Please Mr. Conductor Don't Put Me Off the Train)
Me M12184, Vo 02683, Pan P12184, Pan 25,
RZAu G22211

C-6875 For Sale, a Baby
Me M12262, Vo 02705, Po 9079, RZAu G22211

C-6876 After the Ball
Me M12332, Vo 5474, Cq 7984, ARC 7-06-70

Note: ARC group includes Banner, Oriole, Romeo, Melotone, Perfect; same release number on all five labels. First digit indicates year of release (7 = 1937), middle pair of digits indicates month (05 = May).

RCA Victor, 14 Sept. 1933, New York, NY.

BS-77659-1 Some Little Bug Is Goin' To Get You Some Day

BS-77659-1 Cont.
BB B-5179, MW M-4379, Su 3276, El 2085
BS-77660-1 Long, Long Ago
BB B-5179, MW M-4379, Su 3276, El 2085
BS-77661-1 The First Whippoorwill Song
BB B-8478, Cam CAL-898
BS-77662-1 Two Little Orphans
BB B-4906
BS-77663-1 In the Little Shirt That Mother Made For Me
BB B-5321, MW M-4421, RZAu G22367, Su 3402
BS-77664-1 Three Wishes
BB B-4906
BS-77665-1 Mammy's Precious Baby
BB B-8478
BS-77666-1 Sweet Betsy From Pike
BB B-5321, MW M-4421, Su 3402, RCA LPV-548
BS-77667-1 The House Carpenter
BB B-5255, Su 3338, El 2135
BS-77668-1 Dog and Gun
BB B-5255, Su 3338, El 2135
BS-77669-1 The Old Wooden Rocker
BB B-5201, MW M-4405, Su 3282, El 2091
BS-77670-1 My Mother's Beautiful Hands
BB B-5201, MW M-4405, Su 3282, El 2091

RCA Victor, 14 Feb. 1934, New York, NY.

BS-81383-1 Somebody's Waiting for You
BB B-8410, RZAu G24913
BS-81384-1 The Letter Edged in Black
BB B-5895, RZAu G22499, RCA LPM 6015
BS-81385-1 Little Rosewood Casket
BB B-5895, RZAu G22499
BS-81386-1 The Ship That Never Returned
BB B-5569, RZAu G22339
BS-81387-1 Jimmie Rodger's Life
BB B-5377, MW M-4456, Su 3458
BS-81388-1 The Death of Jimmie Rodgers
BB B-5377, MW M-4456, Su 3458
BS-81389-1 Mrs. Rodgers' Lament
BB B-5423, MW M-4457, RZAu G22367

BS-81390-1 Life Is Like a Mountain Railroad
BB B-8501
BS-81391-1 Little Joe
BB B-5423, MW M-4457
BS-81392-1 The Blind Girl
BB B-8501, RZAu G22339
BS-81393-1 I'll Take You Home Again Kathleen
BB B-5569, RZAu G22339
BS-81394-1 Zeb Tourney's Gal (Feud Song)
BB B-8410

RCA Victor, 7 May 1934, New York, NY.

BS-82388-1 The Death of Jimmie Rodgers
BB B-5486, RCA LSP-4073 (e)
BS-82389-1 The Life of Jimmie Rodgers
BB B-5486, RCA LSP-4073 (e)
BS-82390-1 In the Hills of Old Kentucky
BB B-5971, RZAu G22554
BS-82391-1 Just Plain Folks
BB B-5991, RZAu G22554

Notes: LP titles: Camden CAL-898: *Maple on the Hill and other Old Time Country Favorites*
Victor LPM-6015: *Stars of the Grand Ole Opry*
Victor LSP 4073: *When the Evening Shadows Fall* ("The Life of Jimmie Rodgers" is titled "Jimmie Rodgers' Life" on this LP)
Victor LPV-548: *Native American Ballads*

Decca Record Co., Sept. 1934, New York, NY.

38649 Darlin' Clementine
DeI W4271
38650 In the Hills of Old Kentucky (My Mountain Rose)
Unissued
38651 My Mother's Beautiful Hands
De 5026, DeI W4271
38652 The Old Wooden Rocker
De 5026, DeI W4372
38653 Ain't We Crazy
De 5025

38654 In the Little Shirt that Mother Made for Me
De 5025, DeI W4372

Decca Record Co., ca. 28 Nov. 1934, New York, NY.

39105 Down By the Railroad Track
De 12035

Note: Piano accomp. on sides issued in De 12000 series by Irma F. Kincaid

Decca Record Co., ca. 30 Nov. 1934, New York, NY.

39122 Sweet Inniscarra
De 12035

39123 The Foggy Dew
De 12024

39124 That Tumble Down Shack in Athlone
De 12024

39125 When Irish Eyes Are Smiling
De 12053

39126 The Cowboy's Dream
De 5048

39143 Red River Valley
De 5048

39144 I'd Like To Be in Texas
De 12053

Bullet Recording and Transcription Co., ca. 1944, Nashville, Tenn.

Bradley Kincaid and his Kentucky Mountain Boys. (Note: No master numbers appear on the Bullet label or in the wax.)

Ain't We Crazy
Bul 615

Now the Table's Turned on You
Bul 615

Majestic Record Co., ca. 1945, Nashville, Tenn.

Bradley Kincaid, vocal and guitar. These recordings for Majestic were subsequently issued on the Varsity label, owned by the Wright Record Corp. of Meriden, Conn. Following release on 78 rpm discs in the late 1940s, they were reissued on a 10 inch Varsity LP, in the late 1940s or early 1950s. Although the Mercury releases bear Mercury master numbers, it seems fairly certain that these were taken from the Majestic recordings and issued in ca. 1952. The Design LP appeared in the early 1960s.

T-1014 The Legend of the Robin Red Breast
Maj 6010, Var LP 34, Design DLP-189 and 625, Mer 6169
T-1015 The Blue Tail Fly
Maj 6010, Var 8038, Var LP 34, Design DLP-189 and 625
T-1068 Those Precious Love Letters
Maj 6011, Var LP-34
T-1069 Footprints in the Snow
Var 8038, Var LP 34, Mer 6169
T-1304 Hummingbird Special
Maj 6020, Var LP 34
T-1305 Red Light Ahead
Maj 6018, Var LP 34
T-1306 The Miner's Song
Maj 6018, Var LP 34
T-1307 The Fatal Derby Day
Maj 6020, Var 8041, Var LP 34

Note: Varsity LP 34 is titled *Bradley Kincaid Singing American Ballads and Folk Songs*; Design DLP 189 and 625 is titled *Cowboy!*

Capitol Records, 1950, Springfield, Oh.

These recordings were made at radio station WSSO, which Kincaid then owned, and sent to Capitol. The group accompanying him was "The Whippoorwills" from Dayton.

6597-D3 Red Light Ahead
Cap 1465
6598-D3 Now the Table's Turned on You
Cap 1465
6599-D3 Brush the Dust from that Old Bible
Cap 1276
6600-D3 Legend of the Robin Red Breast
Cap 1276

Bluebonnet Recording Studios, 6-9 Aug. 1963, Fort Worth, Tex.

One Hundred and sixty-two songs were recorded at this four-day recording session, seventy-four of which have been released to date on six LPs, all titled *Mountain Ballads and Old Time Songs.*

Album Number One—Bluebonnet BL 107

Barbara Allen
Billy Boy
Footprints in the Snow
Down In the Valley
The Fatal Derby Day
Four Thousand Years Ago
Methodist Pie
The First Whippoorwill
I Gave My Love a Cherry
I'll Remember You, Love, In My Prayers
The Little Shirt that Mother Made for Me
Liza Up in the 'Simmon Tree
I Love My Rooster
The Legend of the Robin's Red Breast

Album Number Two—Bluebonnet BL 105

The Letter Edged in Black
The Gypsy's Warning
Fingerprints Upon the Window Pane
There's No Place Like Home
In a Village By the Sea
My Grandfather's Clock
My Sweet Iola
Don't Make Me Go to Bed and I'll Be Good
Just Plain Folks
Just as the Sun Went Down
High Grass Town
Two Little Orphans
The Hunters of Kentucky
Life's Railway to Heaven

Album Number Three—Bluebonnet BL 109

In the Hills of Old Kentucky
Bury Me Out on the Prairie
Dog and Gun
I'd Like to Be in Texas
I Wonder When I Shall Be Married
The Blue Tail Fly
The Three Wishes (Or Better Than Gold)
Get Away Old Man, Get Away
The House Carpenter
There's a Red Light Ahead

Album Number Four—Bluebonnet BL 112

Give My Love to Nell
Cindy
The Life of Jimmy Rodgers
The True and Trembling Brakeman

Album Number Four—Cont.

Sweet Kitty Wells
The Wreck on the C & O Road
Only As Far As the Gate
I Loved You Better Than You Knew
The Housekeeper's Tragedy
Pearl Bryan
The Hills of Old New Hampshire
How Beautiful Heaven Must Be

Album Number Five—Bluebonnet BL 118

Molly Darlin'
Night Time in Nevada
Steamboat Bill
Nobody's Darling
How the Banjo Was Invented
Beautiful Dreamer
Those Precious Love Letters
Ain't We Crazy?
Charlie Brooks
Little Brown Jug
Darling Nellie Gray
When Jesus Beckons Me Home

Album Number Six—Bluebonnet BL 123

Little Old Log Cabin in the Lane
Listen to the Mocking Bird
Willie, Down by the Pond
What'll I Do With the Baby-O
The Blind Child
There Was an Old Soldier
My Mother's Old Red Shawl
Little Green Valley
Tildy Johnson
Roll Along, Kentucky Moon
Mary Wore Three Links of Chain
Beautiful Isle of Somewhere

McMonigle Music, Inc., 1973, Springfield, Oh.

On the following songs Kincaid is accompanied by a bluegrass-style band. The LP, *Bradley Kincaid: The Kentucky Mountain Boy*, was issued both as McMonigle BK 101A/102B and Round Robin 101 (on JEMF's copy, the record label name is Round Robin and the jacket name is McMonigle).

On Top of Old Smokey
Letter Edged in Black
Gooseberry Pie
Four Thousand Years Ago
Gypsy's Warning
I Gave My Love a Cherry
I'll Remember You Love, In My Prayers
I Love My Rooster
Footprints in the Snow
In the Little Shirt My Mother Made For Me
The Fatal Derby Day
Life's Railway to Heaven

Round Robin Records (McMonigle), 1973, Springfield, Oh.

LM-104A	There's a Red Light Ahead
LM-104B	Legend of the Robin's Red Breast

Old Homestead Records, Brighton, Mich., 1976

These numbers are reissued from 78 rpm recordings.

Bradley Kincaid. Mountain Ballads and Old-Time Songs, OHCS 107 (Collectors series)

Liza Up a Simmon Tree
Four Thousand Years Ago
Some Little Bug is Going to Get You Some Day
Barbara Allen
The Fatal Wedding
Gooseberry Pie
Two Little Girls in Blue
My Mother's Beautiful Hands
Somebody's Waiting For You
The Blind Child
Give My Love To Nell
The Little Shirt My Mother Made For Me
Ain't We Crazy
After the Ball
Picture From Life's Other Side
Down By the Railroad Track

McMonigle Music, Inc., 1978 (recorded in 1973), Springfield, Oh.

Bradley Kincaid, Family Gospel Album, BK3, BK4

The Old Rugged Cross
There's A Church in the Valley
Showers of Blessing
Where is My Wandering Boy Tonight
Amazing Grace
Beautiful Isle of Somewhere
When Jesus Beckons Me Home
Red Light Ahead
How Beautiful Heaven Must Be
The Unclouded Day
Ninety and Nine
Whispering Hope
Since the Cross Cast Its Shadow on Me
I Am Not Ashamed of Jesus

SOURCES

Books and Articles

Biggar, George C. "Facts on Radio Broadcasting: 1920-1964." DeKalb, Illinois: WLBK-AM & FM (May, 1964), mimeographed paper.

______. "The National Barn Dance." *Country & Western Scrapbook*. Ed. Thurston Moore. 14th edition (no date or location given on material).

Child, Francis James. *The English and Scottish Popular Ballads.* 5 vols. Boston: Houghton Mifflin, 1884-1898; rpt. New York: Dover, 1965.

Derek, Joe. "Bradley Kincaid is a Legend in Grand Old Opryland." Springfield *Sun* (March 24, 1975).

Evans, James F. *Prairie Farmer and WLS: The Burridge D. Butler Years.* Urbana: The University of Illinois Press, 1969.

Ford, Ed. "Bradley Kincaid . . . . The Man Who's Called Country Music's Pioneer." *Berea Alumnus* (January-February, 1975), 5-7.

Green, Archie. "Bradley Kincaid's Folios." *JEMF Quarterly*, 12 (Summer 1977), 21-28.

Henderson, Tom. "Mac Wiseman." *Pickin'* (August, 1975).

Kincaid, Bradley. *Favorite Old Time Songs and Mountain Ballads* (Book No. 3). Chicago: WLS, 1930.

______. *Mountain Ballads: Old Time Songs* (Book No. 8). New York: Southern Music Publishing Company, 1937.

______. *My Favorite Mountain Ballads and Old-Time Songs* (Book No. 5). Pittsburgh: KDKA, 1932.

Malone, Bill C. *Country Music, U. S. A.* Austin: University of Texas Press, 1968.

______. and Judith McCulloh, eds. *Stars of Country Music: Uncle Dave Macon to Johnny Rodriguez*. Urbana: University of Illinois Press, 1975.

"Old Ballad Hits on Radio." Jackson, Mississippi, *News* (September 13, 1929).

Rinzler, Ralph. "Bill Monroe." *Stars of Country Music: Uncle Dave Macon to Johnny Rodriguez*. eds. Bill C. Malone and Judith McCulloh. Urbana: University of Illinois Press, 1975. p. 202-21.

Shelton, Robert, and Burt Goldblatt. *The Country Music Story*. Secaucus, New Jersey: Castle Books, 1966.

Wilgus, D. K. "Bradley Kincaid." *Stars of Country Music: Uncle Dave Macon to Johnny Rodriguez*. eds. Bill C. Malone and Judith McCulloh. Urbana: University of Illinois Press, 1975, pp. 86-94.

Wolfe, Charles. "Grandpa and Ramona Jones: Two Lives, One Music." *The Devil's Box* (December 1, 1979), pp. 3-20.

All editions of Bradley's 12 songbooks were consulted.

Correspondence

Biggar, George C., letter of April 12, 1975.

Cisler, Stephen A., letter of May 17, 1975.

Davis, Karl, letter of April 24, 1975.

Kincaid, Bradley, letter of March 31, 1976.

Malin, Don C., letter of June 5, 1975.

Nesbitt, Eddie, letter of December 28, 1977.

Powell, Reuben, letter of April 24, 1975.

Ralston, J. H., letter of May 22, 1975.

Segal, Clementine Legg, letter of June, 1975.

Troyan, Joe, letter of October 7, 1976.

Wiseman, Scott, letter of April 18, 1975.

Fan letters to Bradley Kincaid. Credit given in text.

Interviews

Anderson, Mr. and Mrs. Clarence J., by Loyal Jones in Berea, Kentucky, July 1, 1977.

Hopkins, Doc, by Sidney Farr in Berea, Kentucky, October 25, 1975.

Kincaid, Bradley, by Dorothy Gable, November 12, 1967 (location unknown). Courtesy of the Country Music Foundation.

Interviews, cont.

Kincaid, Bradley, telephone conversation with Loyal Jones, January 20, 1978.

Kincaid, Bradley, by Loyal Jones in Berea, Kentucky, April 24, 1974.

Kincaid, Bradley, by Reuben Powell in Springfield, Ohio, January 21, 1971.

Kincaid, Bradley, by Ruth Wilson, undated. Courtesy of the Country Music Foundation.

Jones, Louis Marshall, telephone conversation with Loyal Jones, September 21, 1976, and in Berea, Kentucky, October 28, 1978.

Jones, Ramona, telephone conversation with Loyal Jones, September 21, 1976, and in Berea, Kentucky, October 28, 1978.

Lair, John, by Loyal Jones at Renfro Valley, Kentucky, April 30, 1974.

Morris, Jimmy, "Driftwood," by Loyal Jones in Timbo, Arkansas, June 12, 1976.

Ralston, James, by Loyal Jones in Berea, Kentucky, April 28, 1974.

Tallmadge, William H., by Loyal Jones in Berea, Kentucky, 1977.

Williams, Cratis D., by Loyal Jones in Berea, Kentucky, March 19, 1976.